I0560984

Edward Fuller

The dramatic year, 1887-88: brief criticism of important theatrical
events in the United States; with a sketch of the season in London

Edward Fuller

The dramatic year, 1887-88: brief criticism of important theatrical events in the United States; with a sketch of the season in London

ISBN/EAN: 9783337304447

Printed in Europe, USA, Canada, Australia, Japan

Cover: Foto ©ninafisch / pixelio.de

More available books at **www.hansebooks.com**

[1887-88]

BRIEF CRITICISMS OF IMPORTANT THEATRICAL

EVENTS IN THE UNITED STATES

WITH A SKETCH OF THE SEASON IN LONDON

BY WILLIAM ARCHER

EDITED BY

EDWARD FULLER.

BOSTON

TICKNOR AND COMPANY

211 Tremont Street

1889

NOTE.

THE present volume is an attempt to present in a compact and attractive form a critical review of the dramatic season just ended. It is not in any sense complete or chronological, nor is it a continuous account of the history of the American stage within the period mentioned; it is rather a presentation and consideration of the luminous (or non-luminous) points in that history. Such a method has rather obvious merits as well as defects, the former of which, in the opinion of the editor, outweigh the latter. No one can be more fully conscious than he, however, that the execution of his plan, at least so far as his individual work is concerned, falls far below the conception. For those who have kindly aided him by their contributions, he is well aware that he needs to make no such excuse. Without them the book would have been an impossibility, and to them one and all he now and here offers the most cordial thanks. To Mr. William Archer, whose admirably comprehensive view of the London season just ended will add much to the value of the volume, and to Mr. H. M. Ticknor and Mr. G. E. Montgomery, whose co-operation deserves the heartiest acknowledgment, the editor must especially express his gratitude, although his debt is hardly less in degree to Mr. Towse (who has generously given him permission to use two articles of his), Mr. Weeks and Mr. Copeland, the last of whom he has to thank for much assistance which does not appear in the table of contents. It should be said, too, that a portion of the articles included have appeared, though for the most part in a different form, in the *Boston Post*, and two of them in the *New York Evening Post*. But the majority of the contributions have been written exclusively for publication here. The only wish which the editor desires to express in this connection is that "The Dramatic Year" may prove as useful in its way to the stage and to those interested in the drama everywhere, as the excellent *Mirror Annual* has already proved to the same class of readers. It is hardly necessary to add that between the present volume of critical essays and that indispensable chronological record there can be no unfriendly rivalry, since each is independent of, although at the same time supplementary to, the other. Whether or not " The Dramatic Year" shall be an annual publication depends, of course, largely upon the degree of public favour with which this experiment is received. Had performances of light operas and burlesques been included in the editor's plan, the wider scope thus gained might, perhaps, have made this contingency more certain; but that could not have been adequately done without enlarging the book beyond the limits proposed. That there is room for a critical review of such performances, as well as of musical attractions of a higher class, will hardly be disputed.

The editor will count it as a great favour if, during the dramatic season which is now opening, managers will send him complete casts of new productions and dates of opening performances.

Office of the POST,
  15, Milk Street, Boston.

CONTENTS.

Part I.

		PAGE
A GLANCE AT THE PAST SEASON	Howard Malcom Ticknor	1
THE SEASON IN LONDON	William Archer	22
SCENIC ART IN MR. IRVING'S "FAUST"	Lyman H. Weeks	42

Part II.

THE LAST YEAR OF "WALLACK'S"	George Edgar Montgomery	55
THE WALLACK TESTIMONIAL	J. Ranken Towse	64
MR. PALMER'S PRODUCTIONS	George Edgar Montgomery	70
"THE WIFE" AT THE LYCEUM	Editor	79
DALY'S THEATRE	George Edgar Montgomery	82
THE BOSTON THEATRE SHOW-PIECES	Howard Malcom Ticknor	92
THE BOSTON MUSEUM	Editor	100
MR. HARRIGAN'S LATEST PLAY	C. T. Copeland	122
A DRAMA OF ANARCHY	J. Ranken Towse	125
WALL STREET ON THE STAGE	Lyman H. Weeks	132
"LA TOSCA"	Editor	139

Part III.

		PAGE
MDME. JANAUSCHEK . .	*Editor* . . .	. 147
THE TWO TRAGEDIANS, BOOTH AND BARRETT .	*Howard Malcom Ticknor* .	157
MR. IRVING IN AMERICA .	*Editor* . . .	· 164
SOME SHAKSPERIAN REVIVALS	*Editor* . . .	. 193
MR. BOUCICAULT AND IRISH DRAMA	*C. T. Copeland* . .	. 208
DOUBLE LIVES IN DRAMA .	*Howard Malcom Ticknor* .	218
MISS MORRIS IN "RENÉE DE MORAY" . . .	*C. T. Copeland* . .	. 225
MR. FREDERICK WARDE .	*C. T. Copeland* . .	. 229
ENGLISH COMEDY BY MISS VOKES	*Editor* . . .	. 232
"A POSSIBLE CASE" . .	*George Edgar Montgomery*	238
MR. SOTHERN'S FIRST TOUR	*C. T. Copeland* .	. 242
SOME MINOR PLAYS . .	*Editor* . . .	. 248
AMBITIOUS AMATEURS . .	*R. E. Woolf* . .	. 258

TIIE DRAMATIC YEAR.

PART I.

A GLANCE AT THE PAST SEASON.

DURING the dramatic season of 1887-88 the almost omnivorous Boston appetite for amusement required the constant attention of eleven places of theatrical entertainment. Of these eight were theatres proper, the others being dime-museums and the like, at which farces and small comedies were regularly presented in every programme by stock companies, which changed their pieces at least once each week.

If the population of Boston seems to be thus over-supplied with dramatic shows, one has only to re-member that not only do all the towns within a radius of ten or fifteen miles, served by late evening trains, furnish a considerable proportion of every audience, but that, during all important engagements, spectators come from Providence, Worcester, Springfield, and other comparatively distant places, often ignoring at home the very companies and plays which they subsequently make journeys to see.

The season began on August 13, 1887—a Saturday

evening, which is in itself an unusual circumstance—
when the Emily Soldene Burlesque and Novelty
Company appeared at the Howard Athenæum.
The regular Monday openings fell on the evening of
August 15, when the McNish, Johnson and Slavin
Minstrels performed at the Globe, and the Leonzo
Brothers' Dramatic Company at the Windsor, where
also there was an afternoon performance. The
Museum—which had had a short miscellaneous summer season—began its forty-seventh regular course
on August 29th, with "The Dominie's Daughter,"
and the other houses followed thus: on September
5th, the Boston Theatre, with the fourteenth annual
selection of "Kit" (Mr. Henry T. Chanfrau) as its
initial attraction; the Park, with the Madison Square
Company in "Jim the Penman," and the Hollis
Street, with the reconstructed and embellished burlesque, "The Corsair," given under Mr. E. E. Rice's
management. The Grand Opera House was announced to be ready for the public in October, but
the work of construction went on so slowly that this
theatre was not opened until January 9th, 1888.
These seasons—with the exception of the last—
averaged from forty-one to forty-two weeks each; the
Howard being the longest and the Grand Opera
House the shortest. At the time when these pages
are written—early in June—the Boston Museum is
occupied by the magician Kellar, who will be followed
by Corinne and Mr. Roland Reed; the Boston
Theatre is open for the Swedish comedienne, Miss
Ullie Akerstrom, in melodramatic pieces; the Park
is assigned for a fortnight to Mr. James A. Herne,

for his new temperance play, " Drifting Apart," and the Howard Athenæum is in the hands of an extra company for a week of Mr. Charles S. Gayler's " Lights and Shadows."

The range of performances, which must be counted by thousands in the regular theatres alone, touched the very extremes, and rested, as it swung to and fro, upon almost every intermediate degree,—the one remarkable omission being that of the Gilbert and Sullivan opera, not a single representation of which, in whole or in part, was anywhere attempted. There is no need of dwelling in detail upon the shows presented by some managers ; while others, again, will receive in special articles the extended comment they merited.

The Windsor, which caters to the roughest and most uncultivated audiences in the city, gave as usual two performances each day, that of the afternoon being always attended by great numbers of children, whose presence, like their possession of even the small sum required for admission, it is not easy to account for. These performances consisted for the most part of wild and improbable melodramas, rampant frontier pieces, and horse-play comedies, alternating with minstrel and variety shows. The manner of these performances was usually on the same common plane as their material, and the staging cheap and often insufficient, although sometimes showily and crudely effective and always accepted by an unfastidious public.

The Howard Athenæum, appealing also to " popu-

lar " tastes, had a similar schedule of entertainments ;
but as the prices of the house are higher and the
patronage of the well-to-do and respectable middle
classes is sought, the prevailing tone is better and
purer. The staging here is almost invariably adequate
when governed by the house management, and the
visiting companies were generally of sufficient standing and means to give good things of their kind with
properly balanced casts and appropriate accessories.
Among the principal actors who appeared were :—
Mr. Louis Aldrich, in " My Partner ;" Mr. Edwin
Arden, in " Eagle's Nest ;" Mr. James C. Roach, a
new and good Irish actor, in " Don Darcy ; " Mr. W.
N. Powers, in " The Ivy Leaf ;" Miss Ada Grey, in
' East Lynne ;" Mr. Gus. Williams, in " Keppler's
Fortunes;" and Mr. McKee Rankin, in " The New
Danites." Among the combinations were the strong
and attractive company organized by the managers
of the house itself, Miss Emily Soldene's, Mr. Tony
Pastor's, " The Night Owls," the Rentz-Santley,
Kernell's, Marinelli's, and Miss Lily Clay's.   One
solitary attempt was made to present the " legitimate," when Mr. Edmund Collier made his first
appearance as a star in Boston.   He presented
" Virginius," " Damon and Pythias," " Metamora,"
" Jack Cade," and " Richard III. ; " but although
he showed many personal qualifications for these
robust rôles, and used them with discretion, his
support was so insufficient and the temper of the
audiences so unsympathetic, that his efforts to set
up standard drama here must be accounted unsuccessful.

The three ten-cent houses—Austin and Stone's Dime Museum, the World's Museum, and the New Gaiety and Bijou—can be passed over in a few words. Each gives a "continuous performance," from ten o'clock in the morning until 10.30 in the evening, the performers appearing in rotation, at intervals of about three hours, and at the first two establishments, curiosities and "freaks" of various kinds are to be seen. A small extra charge is made for reserved seats ; but the two fees nowhere amount to more than twenty-five cents. Mr. B. T. Keith has preserved the original decorations of the Bijou Theatre, and has increased the available space by taking possession of a large ground-floor hall, which has been handsomely ornamented in a harmonious style. As his house is the largest and best, and does not depend upon accessory exhibitions, his entertainments are the best of their kind, and the farces which go with them are often very well acted, as the small company is led by Mr. John Barker, who is a capital comedian of an old-fashioned, but commendable style. The general aspect of his audiences is also better.

Turning now to the other houses, which confine themselves almost entirely to substantial pieces of dramatic or musical character—substantial, at least, in the number of their acts, the numerousness of their casts, and the elaboration of their mountings, a few large results and suggestive considerations present themselves for notice and remembrance.

About 160 different plays were produced at these theatres ; and if there be added to the list those given at the Howard and the Windsor, a total of about 230 will be found. Of these over sixty were new to Boston, four were new to America, and one was given for the first time. The Museum headed the list of novelties to America with three plays, secured abroad by Mr. Field,—"The Red Lamp," by Outram Tristram; "The Soggarth," by George Darrell; and "The Bells of Haslemere," by Henry Pettitt and Augustus Harris,—and added three pieces not previously seen in Boston, viz. "The Dominie's Daughter," by David D. Lloyd; "Sophia," dramatized by Robert Buchanan, after incidents in Fielding's "Tom Jones," and "Dandy Dick," by A. W. Pinero. The Hollis Street, however, brought out the one absolute novelty in Mr. Boucicault's "Cuishla-ma-Chree," which had nothing but the name of novelty to commend it, being only a thin and ineffective paraphrase of the old drama, founded upon "Guy Mannering."

The Museum, nobly adhering to its traditions and habits, depended for nearly the entire season upon its stock company, in the composition of which a few changes had been made from previous seasons; but by no means so many as are promised for that which is come. For some months the plays presented met with less patronage than their own merits and the care bestowed upon their production deserved, an indefinable something in each interrupting the current of mutual sympathy between the theatre and the public. In "The Dominie's Daughter," the illogical and unpleasant ending no doubt alienated liking, and this was modified too late, after the general verdict had set against the piece. The English plays did not fit the American taste, and had but brief runs ; " The Red Lamp " had owed its London favour to the exceptional power of one man, and " Dandy Dick " had been a failure with Mr. Augustin Daly, by whose company, however, it is understood to have been less well played than here in Boston, Miss Clarke particularly having surpassed Miss Rehan as *Mrs. Tidman.*

By way of offset to these pieces, there were interpolated revivals of " The Barrister," " The Magistrate," " Simpson & Co.," " Still Waters Run Deep," " A Scrap of Paper," and two or three smaller pieces, these running for three or six nights, or being put up as the special attractions of single evenings.

At last, on February 6th, Mr. Field reached " The Bells of Haslemere," which he mounted carefully and prettily, and to which he gave a strong cast, there being specially engaged Miss Miriam O'Leary, Miss Maida Craigen and Mr. F. W. Sidney, of London, son of Mr. William Sidney, Stage Manager of the Adelphi, London, who came over in order to assist in staging the play. This drama immediately took the public fancy, and its run extended to eighty performances, being next to that of " A Run of Luck " at the Boston Theatre, and almost double that of " Sophia," which was second in importance here. The play would easily have finished out the season, but contracts had been made with Mdme. Janauschek and Mr. Mansfield, which compelled a withdrawal on the afternoon of April 14th, the evening having been assigned to Mr. Wilson for his benefit. Mdme. Janauschek expected to fill her three weeks with "Meg Merrilies," in which her impersonation of the old nurse had made a notable impression; but the public did not sustain her, and she occupied her third week with "Bleak House," taking a testimonial benefit on the Saturday evening as *Lady Macbeth.* Mr. Mansfield's engagement was fashionable, and amply patronized. He played his usual repertory—"Prince Karl," "A Parisian Romance," and "Dr. Jekyll and Mr. Hyde,"—to which he added his last construction, "Monsieur," which did not meet with much acceptance, and was withdrawn after a week. During the first three weeks he had the support of the Museum company, and then that of his own people. "The Bells of Haslemere," interrupted in the height of its popularity, was only laid aside for the summer, and will be revived at the beginning of the next season.

After the withdrawal of "A Run of Luck," which had filled nearly three months, the management of the Boston Theatre put on for a fortnight a revival of "The Exiles," and then surrendered the house, as usual, to various combinations for various terms. Here were played Mr. Irving's engagement of four weeks, and that of Messrs. Booth and Barrett, which lasted two weeks, and which together marked the highest point in art and in conscientious devotion reached during the season, the "Julius Cæsar" of the latter ranking in care and intelligent intention, although not in minuteness and in expense, with the former's "Olivia" and "Faust." Mr. Irving also won much respect by the scrupulous completeness of detail and simple elegance with which he mounted the sketchy "Jingle," as well as obtaining much praise for the easy humour which he infused into the *title-rôle*.

The only other tragedy seen on this stage was supplied by the turgid and artificial impersonations of Miss Mather, who played for a week in "Leah," and "Romeo and Juliet," contrasting these with the strange mixture of grace and extravagance which constitutes her comedy in "The Honeymoon" and "As You Like It."

Minor engagements were those with the McNish, Johnson, and Slavin, and the Thatcher, West and Primrose Minstrels; Mr. Emmett, in "Fritz;" Messrs. Murray and Murphy in "Our Irish Visitors;" Miss Cora Tanner in "Alone in London," and with Mr. Denman Thompson, who played "The Old Homestead" for a week in December, and again for a fortnight in the spring. The last week of the season was occupied by a revival of "The World."

At intervals during the season there also came Mr. Bandmann, who, returning to the house where he had won success as a classic actor in earlier years, now made a sensation with his version of "Dr. Jekyll and Mr. Hyde;" the Bolossy Kiralfy company in a well-managed spectacle called "Dolores," built up out of Sardou's "Patrie," and adorned with ballet-dancing, juggling, and singing; the National Opera Company, whose always highly commendable and often quite perfect performances, especially of such new works as "The Queen of Sheba," "Nero," "Tannhäuser," were treated with a contumacious neglect incomprehensible by any one who does not know how little right Bostonians have to boast of being intelligent and catholic friends of music and musical enterprise; the Boston Ideals, whose unequal performances were chiefly sustained by the personal attractiveness and professional cleverness of Miss De Lussan, whom Miss Helen Dudley Campbell, as the contralto, well supported; and the Bostonians, whose well-balanced forces and excellent choice of interesting operas had a great success.

The Park Theatre occupied most of its season with farcical plays, which always seem strangely out of place in this cosy house, where fine domestic drama and high comedy can be seen and heard to such advantage. The whole series of Hoyt plays, from the "Rag Baby" down to the "Hole in the Ground," were given, and other contributions of similar rank were made by Miss Myra Goodwin in "Philopene," Lotta in "Pawn Ticket Number 210," an idiotic jumble given for the first time (and I hope the last) in Boston; Mr. Sol Smith Russell, in "Bewitched;" Mr. Gillette in "The Private Secretary;" Mr. N. C. Goodwin, in "Turned Up," a piece new to Boston, and far too redolent of disgusting drunkenness; and Messrs. Gilbert, Donnelly and Girard, with Miss Amy Ames, in "Natural Gas," the one acceptable part of which was Miss Ames's impersonation of an old Irishwoman. The revival of the "Rag Baby" had special interest for its public because Mr. Charles Reed, leaving minstrelsy and comic opera, took the part of *Old Sport*, while the base-ball player, Mr. M. J. Kelly, took that of *Dusty Bob*.

Better comedy—indeed, comedy that often touches the best in the "character" line—was that of Mr. and Mrs. W. J. Florence, who filled a week with "Our Governor," "The Mighty Dollar," "Dombey and Son," "The Flirt," and Mr. B. E. Woolf's new version of his own "Husband Hunting." Nor must the sparkling and unaffected humour and keen point of the little plays acted by Miss Vokes and her small but capable company pass unremembered here.

About midway in the season Colonel McCaull occupied four weeks with light operas, which he presented with a finer group of accomplished vocalists than any of his predecessors had done, and caused the orchestra, chorus, and staging to be all excellent also. He gave "Boccaccio," "Bellman," which was new here, "Falka," and the trashy and uninteresting "Begum" of Messrs. De Koven and Smith. Mdme. Cottrelly, Miss Manola, Mrs. Joyce-Bell, and Messrs Wilke, Bell, De Wolf Hopper, De Angelis, Macdonough and Hoff were prominent in the casts, and Mr. Nowak was the conductor.

In April a fortnight was given for the revised and greatly improved version of "Held by the Enemy," in which the author, Mr. Gillette, assumed the part of the war correspondent, and the season was ended, as it had been begun, with dignity and elegance, by Mr. A. M. Palmer's Madison Square Company. Of

this last engagement two weeks were allowed for
" Partners," which did not begin to please Boston as
it had pleased New York, to Mr. Palmer's surprise,
one week was taken by " Elaine," which was wholly
admired by the only moderately large audiences
which it attracted, and three weeks were given to
" Jim the Penman," which crowded the house at
every repetition. The main features of these plays
were the ever-admirable acting of Mrs. Agnes Booth-
Schoeffel as *Nina Ralston;* the growing mastery of
the English language shown by Mr. Salvini, as well
as of his own personal resources, which, however,
were still too exuberantly used in " Partners;" the
real queenliness of beauty and demeanour in Miss
Burrough's *Guinevere;* the tranquil tenderness of Miss
Russell's *Elaine;* and the repetition of their former
successes by Miss Harrison, Mr. Robinson, Mr. Holland and Mrs. Phillips. Mr. Palmer staged his
pieces handsomely; the banking-house scene in
" Partners," and the funeral-barge tableaux in
" Elaine," were memorably done.

The season at the Globe was one of much variety,
but of rather low average in merit and importance.
There were three engagements which deserved
respect—that of Mrs. Barry and Mr. Redmund, who
gave in excellent style their new romantic piece,
" René;" that of Mr. Jefferson, who brought out
" Rip Van Winkle," " The Cricket on the Hearth,"
and " Lend me Five Shillings;" and that of Miss
Clara Morris, who came in unusual strength and gave
an impressive embodiment of the heroine in Clinton

Stuart's "Renée de Moray," a version of D'Ennery's "La Martyre." The society amateurs had two innings—once when Mrs. Langtry introduced to Boston "As in a Looking-Glass," walking through it in her usual fashion, and dying with extravagant gymnastics, and replaced it with "A Wife's Peril," and again when Mrs. James Brown Potter's pretty incompetence was, shown in Ross Neil's poor play of "Loyal Love." These ladies were respectively supported by the artificiality of Mr. Barrymore and the affectation of Mr. Bellew, and neither held large audiences all through her stay, although some nights saw crowds in attendance.

The sensational and spectacular schools were represented by Mr. Fred Bryton, who seems to be worth something better, in "Forgiven," which got him, during two engagements, great applause and patronage ; Mr. O'Neill in "Monte Cristo ;" Imre Kiralfy's company in "Lagardére," an embellished edition of "The Duke's Motto ;" the Hill and Richardson company in "Lights of London ;" Mr. Mansfield in his usual repertory, to which he added one performance—the first in Boston—of "Monsieur;" Mr. Scanlan in "Shane-na-Lawn ;" Mr. Murphy in "Kerry Gow," &c. ; the Hanlans in "Un Voyage en Suisse," and "Fantasma."

Two productions belonging to this class should be mentioned separately. One was the Imre Kiralfy spectacle of "Mazulm, the Night Owl," which, although almost utterly unlike the original Ravel pantomime which it purported to revive, had so much ingenuity, spirit, and effectiveness as to make a great success. Several gymnastic specialities were introduced, and there was given as an *entre-acte* a remarkable act upon a revolving double trapeze, by the two Vaidis sisters, the younger of whom afterward plunged from the height of the ceiling into a net spread across the orchestra seats. The other was " A Dark Secret," in which the tank, the latest successor of the architectural staircase in popular favour, occupied a large part of the stage and of public attention. The theme received some respect on account of its hoary age, and the unquestionably well-managed realism of the boats and birds which moved over the great expanse of water, and the suspense incident to the attempted drowning and ultimate rescue of the heroine, explained the enthusiasm with which the drama was followed up even by that class of the public which rarely looks upon a melodrama.

Operatic performances were fairly given in French by Mr. Grau's company during a single week. " La Grande Mogul " (new here), " Le Serment d'Amour," and some familiar works were sung, the best artists being Mdmes. Bennati and Pirard, and MM. Guernoy, Mezierès, and Maris. " Erminie," given by the Casino Company, with Misses Pauline Hall, Marie Jansen and Cheatham, and Messrs. Wilson, Daboll, Olmi, Plunkett and Hallam in the caste, asserted its power by drawing full houses for a month ; and later on Mr. Aronson's second company, including Misses Ricci, Urquhart, Grubb and Gerrish, and Messrs. Pounds, Tams, Mark Smith and James T. Powers, gave, for two weeks each, " Madelon," and " The Marquis," both operas being new to Boston, and staged and performed according to the original New York standards.

Burlesque showed itself in its most elaborate and gorgeous form in a week of " The Corsair," which returned to Boston after the winter's voyaging ; it was fairly commendable in " Little Puck," a dramatization for Mr. Frank Daniels (previously noted for his *Old Sport*), which had apparently required for its exhaustive absurdity the co-operation of four playwrights, Messrs. A. C. Gunter, F. C. Maeder, R. Frazer, and H. P. Taylor ; and it came perilously near the lowest line above absolute vulgarity in Ezra Kendall's " Pair of Kids," and W. S. Mestayer's " Check 44, or Tobogganning."

A pleasant interlude there was of a single week, during which the magician Herrmann presented a brilliant entertainment, in which he incorporated the new French trick, " Le Cocon," and a series of illusions done in a black-hung chamber and grouped under the name of " The Black Art."

The Hollis Street, while yielding a little to the demands of that commoner public which wants " knockabout " farces and coarsish dramas, generally furnished entertainment of an excellent character and often gave weeks of the very best. Its least meritorious production was Mr. McNally's " Upside Down," a common and uproarious protracted farce, written to suit the capabilities of the uncultivated and acrobatic Dalys, who greatly gratified their particular following by their antics, and absolutely obtained for themselves a return engagement. Still in the line of "popular" pieces, but of a higher grade, were :— Mrs. McKee Rankin's "Golden Giant," a mining-camp play, rebuilt upon the lines of "Gabriel Conroy," Mr. Gillette's dramatization of "She," and Justin Adams's version of "Dawn." All these were new to Boston, and being judiciously cast and mounted with due regard to effect, although by no means lavishly, did each a good business in its turn. Miss Minnie Palmer also contributed her new and ridiculous play, written by Leonard Grover, called "My Brother's Sister," and quite beneath serious criticism, in which her taking ways and her inconsistent display of jewels proved as usual efficient to attract large audiences. Mr. Edward Harrigan brought his company to fill the last two weeks of the season. He began with "Pete," for which the public cared little, although he was good in an *Uncle Tom* sort of part, and replaced it with "Old Lavender," which drew well.

The really important events of the season illustrated nearly all accepted departments of stage-work. First there was the remodelled "Corsair," which Mr. Rice put on with a great deal of resplendence and parade, and with considerable taste, having collected a company of favourites, among whom were Misses Summerville, Montague, Rose Cooke and Uart, and Messrs. Brocolini, Schiller and David. The music was trivial and tinkling, the scenes and costumes showy, and there was a full array of pretty-faced and huge-limbed women. Mr. Rice went through the motions of directing the first performance, and the burlesque ran vigorously for six weeks. Mr. Bouci-

cault, bringing his own support, played two engagements, during which his old pieces, such as " The
Shaughraun " and " The Colleen Bawn," did much
better for the theatre than his new " Phryne," and
" Cuishla Ma Chree." Mr. E. H. Sothern played two
engagements with " The Highest Bidder," adding to
it on his return, " Editha's Burglar," which latter
piece had been previously presented by Mr. Gillette
when he came with Mdme. De Naucaze to give " The
Great Pink Pearl." These three pieces were all new
to Boston, and they all made a good impression ;
the last was of rather flimsy texture, but it was worth
at least as much in general estimation as the " Railroad of Love," with which Mr. Augustin Daly filled
the brilliant week of his company's visit. Comic
opera had a two weeks' course, when Mr. Duff's
company gave as a novelty, " Dorothy," with Misses
Lillian Russell, Agnes Stone, Leighton and Halton,
and Messrs. Oudin, Brand, Paulton and Hamilton.
Mr. Frederick Warde, a young actor, with evident
qualifications for the robustly romantic drama, played
a good engagement of a week, and was praised ; his
bills were, " Damon and Pythias," " Galba " (a version
of " The Gladiator,") and " Gaston Cadol," a thing
very like " The Lady of Lyons " in plan and result.
Miss Eugenie Blair was more than acceptable as his
leading lady. Messrs. Robson and Crane occupied
four weeks with their famous "Henrietta," and the
artistic height of the season was attained during the
engagement of Mdme. Modjeska, who devoted her
talent and that of an excellent company almost
entirely to Shakespeare, reviving for the first time in

c

many years, " Measure for Measure," and "Cymbeline."

A new theatre was opened, after many promises
and delays on January 9th, 1888. Constructed on
the site and within the walls of the old Columbian
skating-rink, it is a fine, convenient, and spacious
playhouse, and seems likely to thrive. The plans of
construction were sketched in New York, but the
responsibility of virtually all the work fell upon Mr.
George Snell—of the firm of Snell and Greyerson—
the architect of Boston Music Hall. The entrances,
lobbies, and staircases are broad and clear, the pitch
of the floor such that the line of sight is everywhere
unobstructed, the immense galleries have a splendid
sweep, and the boxes are airy and ample. Ventila-
tion, warmth, and safety all had due consideration,
and the ornamentation is done for the most part
directly upon the solid brick exterior or division
walls. The stage, of which all the dimensions are
ample, is built with modern conveniences, but the
drop-curtain is not to be praised. although it is not
so violent in colour or so bad in drawing as some
others in town. The proprietors and managers,
Messrs. Proctor and Mansfield, established a moderate scale of prices, and announced their intention of
catering only to the highest taste ; but the attractions thus far presented cannot be classed above the
"popular" level. The only engagement which had
interest for "society" was that of Miss Maude Banks,
who played a week in her own "Joan of Arc,"
manifesting a distinct ability and an equally distinct

need of critical training. The opening attraction
was a version of the story of Aladdin, called " The
Arabian Nights," and presented for three weeks by
the Imperial Burlesque Company in a dashing but
not elegant fashion. Subsequent weeks brought out
such " emotional " plays as " Her Atonement,"
" Hoodman Blind," " Beacon Lights," " The Silver
King," " The Streets of New York," " Zitka,"
" Under the Gaslight," " Michael Strogoff," &c.,
while the standard of a first-class theatre was entirely set aside in the weeks assigned for " Peck's
Bad Boy," " Two Old Cronies," and the Australian
Novelty Company's specialty performance. Mr. C.
L. Davis gave a Yankee week in " Alvin Joslyn,"
Mr. Charles T. Ellis, one of Dutch comedy and sing-
ing in " Casper the Yodler," and Miss Minnie Maddern
acted for a week in " Caprice," and " In Spite of All."

Signor Campanini, unable to obtain the Boston
Theatre, took this house for the three representations
of Verdi's " Otello," which he had assigned to Boston,
and was quite unrewarded for his enterprise. Generously and handsomely mounted, cast in nearly every
respect with high ability—for Signore Tetrazzini and
Scalchi and Signori Galassi and Campanini sang the
principal parts—and supplied with full and competent orchestra and chorus, the opera was almost absolutely neglected by those people of Boston who
make most profession of their love for music and
their knowledge of it. The artists were faithfulness
itself, however, singing and acting as though their
audiences were crowded and remunerative, and received intelligent and liberal applause in return.

At the present writing the house is promised for a couple of weeks to the Wilbur Opera Company, and, as other attractions are underlined, the inference is that it may continue open during the summer.

All things considered, it may be doubted whether the season of 1887-88 has been a very prosperous one for the managers. The lower order of pieces have drawn, of course, for they appeal to an enormous number of people, who do not divide their attention between this and other sorts of amusements. But discriminating people have now many claims upon their attention, their time, and their money, and they do not really frequent the theatres, although in the course of the season they sample everything, so to speak. So exceptional an inducement as a visit from Mr. Irving brings them together in force for successive evenings, but during the best of other engagements, while one would find that a great many people noted for culture or position had been at the theatre, he would still observe but few at any one representation. Hence it is probably that return engagements of any but the greatest favourites are comparatively ill rewarded, and that few patrons repeat their visits to any play, unless perhaps it be something like "Jim the Penman," "The Henrietta," or a Daly comedy.

Apart from the farces of various lengths, the evenly cast and well-mounted comedies have probably averaged best, as produced by companies of permanent composition, and the almost universal voice has been in favour of the work thus done. The English plays will not all suit American audiences, any more than the English apprehension can " catch on " to American humour, and the smallest successes of the season have been made in imported dramas, as, on the other hand, some foreign pieces have been greatly successful.

As a whole, Boston has held its own very well, in giving people a chance to become acquainted with approved novelties and in maintaining one good, well-built, stock company. It must be admitted, however, that Boston has something to learn from New York in nicety and delicacy of staging and scene-painting, the latter of which, although usually good in design, seems hard, crude, and bald beside the work of the New York artists. It is not possible, perhaps, for a Boston manager, who cannot hope for anything like the transient patronage of the metropolis, and can only expect a few weeks' run instead of a whole season, to have as costly things or as many of them as a New York manager, but taste and feeling are independent of the price of canvas, paint, furniture, and upholstery, and many beautiful effects are found in comparatively inexpensive settings which come to Boston on their rounds. It is worth while for the local managers to consider this and to make an effort for greater elegance and style, now that the comparison with New York is brought up fifty times in a season. Boston cannot afford the highest-priced luxuries of the stage for her own home consumption, but she can be as dainty and refined as any city if she chooses.

HOWARD MALCOM TICKNOR.

THE SEASON IN LONDON.

[1887-88.]

THE theatrical life of London has no period of utter stagnation, or, as Dr. Holmes would say, of "æstivation," between season and season. There are always some half-dozen theatres open, and the occurrence of a Bank Holiday early in August sometimes tempts our melodramatic managers to venture an important production just at the time when in Paris, and, I believe, in America, things are at their very dullest. This was the case last season. The Brothers Gatti, dealers in macaroni and melodrama at the Adelphi, produced on Thursday, July 28th, 1887, "The Bells of Haslemere," by Messrs. Henry Pettitt and Sydney Grundy; and from this point I propose to start in my review of the theatrical year.

As a melodrama meets us on the threshold, let me give melodrama the precedence over higher and more interesting art-forms—business first, pleasure afterwards. "The Bells of Haslemere" was looked forward to with some curiosity, as it was Mr. Sydney Grundy's first attempt in popular drama of this description, and some of us were sanguine enough to hope that he might make the puppets dance to a new tune. Alas! it was not to be. There was little trace of Mr.

Grundy's handiwork in the play. He may have blown
the bellows, but Mr. Pettitt certainly worked the keys,
and banged out the old, old tune in the old, old style.
The result was, of course, a great success, and a run
of nearly 300 nights, during which the Messrs. Gatti
managed somehow to rebuild their theatre, giving it
a showy front upon the Strand, and greatly enlarging
the pit. The pit at the Adelphi is the goose that lays
the golden eggs. Next on the melodramatic list we
have "The Pointsman," an over-complicated but not
ill-written play by Messrs. Carton and Raleigh, at the
Olympic, and "Pleasure," by Messrs. Paul Merritt and
Augustus Harris, at Drury Lane. Mr. Harris lavished
all his skill as a stage-manager on a picture of the
carnival at Nice, and on a moral earthquake which
came along just in the nick of time to clear the
heroine's character and cure the hero of an unwise
partiality for brandy-and-soda—thus "justifying the
ways of God to man." At Christmas-time Mr. Wilson
Barrett, returning from his American and provincial
tour, opened the Globe Theatre with a new melodrama
by himself and Mr. G. R. Sims, entitled "The Golden
Ladder." In this Mr. Barrett appeared in the only
too congenial character of a parson ; the French navy
was wantonly insulted in an episodic act located in
Madagascar ; and Miss Eastlake played with heart-
rending realism in a painful prison-scene towards the
close. It was absolutely the worst play Mr. Sims
ever wrote, which is saying a good deal ; and it was
but moderately successful. In the meantime, Miss
Grace Hawthorne, who, as my readers may be surprised
to learn, is understood to be a distinguished American

actress, was pursuing her chequered career of management in Mr. Barrett's old theatre, the Princess's. "The Shadows of a Great City," very fairly played, was a success; Mr. Bartley Campbell's "Siberia" was an utter failure; and "The Mystery of a Hansom Cab," a rough-and-ready adaptation of an Australian "shilling shocker," was industriously advertised into a fair imitation of success. An arrangement was now come to between Miss Hawthorne and Mr. Wilson Barrett, by which the latter returned to his old abode to produce a new play, entitled "The Ben My Chree," adapted from Mr. Hall Caine's Manx novel, "The Deemster." Mr. Hall Caine is a young man of picturesque exterior, who tended the dying years, or rather months, of Dante Gabriel Rossetti, wrote a book of reminiscences of that extraordinary genius, and has since devoted himself to the production of Hugoesque romances, of which "The Deemster" is the latest. Produced at the Princess's Theatre last May, "The Ben My Chree" was recognized as a far stronger piece of work than the average melodrama, though it scarcely rose, as Mr. Caine would have us believe, to the dignity of tragedy. The first three acts were interesting, novel, and to a certain extent poetic; the last two, unfortunately, were very feeble, and ruined the play—financially, I believe, as well as artistically. A glance at the Olympic will complete the melodramatic record. Here, under Mr. Yorke Stephens' management, Messrs. Percy Lynwood and Mark Ambient produced a preposterous Nihilistic drama entitled "Christina," which they ran for several weeks, in spite of critical condemnation and public

neglect. It was succeeded by Mr. Rutland Barrington's adaptation of that much-advertised novel "Mr.
Barnes of New York," in which Mr. Willard, who so
long played the villain to Mr. Barrett's heroes at the
Princess's, created the part of *Count Danella*. The
play had only a short run, and it cannot be said that
this season has dispersed the cloud of ill-luck which
has so long brooded over the Olympic. In sum, then,
we have this year had one melodrama, "The Bells of
Haslemere," which deserved to fail, but succeeded,
and one, "The Ben My Chree," which deserved to
succeed, and practically failed. The rest are of no
account, either in respect of intrinsic merit or of
popularity.

One great feature of the past season has been the
preponderance of the American element in our
theatrical life. I have already spoken of Miss
Hawthorne at the Princess's, who, if not a distinguished American, is at least an American, *sans
phrase*, and has dealt largely in American wares.
The beginning of the period I am reviewing saw the
close of Mrs. Brown-Potter's mismanaged and melancholy attempt to take the English stage by storm.
I am myself one of those who admire this lady's
pluck, and do not deny her the possession of considerable talent in a more or less crude state; but an
angel from heaven could not have succeeded in the
characters she essayed. After the failure of "Civil
War" at the Gaiety, she produced "Loyal Love," a
blank-verse play by "Ross Neil," a prolific, but un-
actable lady dramatist, who died a few weeks ago.
It was pitiful to see Mrs. Brown-Potter struggling so

earnestly with such hopeless material — and to empty benches. Scarcely had Mrs. Brown-Potter retreated from the Gaiety when Miss Mary Anderson opened her winter campaign at the Lyceum. She had already produced "The Winter's Tale" at Notting-ham, and had played it once or twice in other provincial towns; but to the immense majority of London playgoers it was practically a novelty. Croaking critics declared that the play never had succeeded, and never could succeed; forgetting that it was one of the chief triumphs of Charles Kean's management at the Princess's, and that it had never since had anything like a fair chance. There were weak points not a few in Miss Anderson's production. Her Hermione, for example, was sadly imperfect. She wantonly maltreated Shakspere's verse, and was inclined to scold in passages where she should have preserved the loftiest self-restraint. Even in this character, however, she had memorable moments of majesty and beauty, while her *Perdita* was an unforgettable creation. I have seen nothing lovelier than her dance in the Pastoral scene, and she spoke the lines of the part with a perfect feeling for their human significance, if not for their literary exquisiteness. Mr. Forbes Robertson was an excellent *Leontes*, and, in spite of its many blemishes, the general impression left by the performance was distinctly pleasant. The critics, who have never had a good word for Miss Anderson, spoke very disdain-fully of the production; but the public rallied faithfully round its favourite, and filled the theatre from September until Easter. The public was surely right

and the critics wrong. We are not so rich in Shake-
spearean acting that we can afford to despise a very
beautiful performance because it is not "a poem,
round and perfect as a star." The departure of Miss
Anderson from the Lyceum was speedily followed
by the arrival of the Daly Company at the Gaiety.
At first the luck ran somewhat against these admirable comedians, whose former visits have established
them firmly in the esteem of the London public.
They opened in "The Railroad of Love," a piece of
slight construction, and full of local allusions unsuited
for exportation. Moreover, some accidental circumstances disposed the first-night audience unfavourably.
The curtain was rung up so very punctually that the
stalls were half empty until the first act was nearly
over, so that many of the critics failed to understand
the plot, and are asking to this day what it was all
about. Their bewilderment was increased by the
fact that the actors took some time to get the proper
pitch of the theatre, and to make themselves distinctly audible. The result was that the press pooh-
poohed the play, though ample justice was done to
the acting of Miss Rehan and Mr. John Drew. The
public gathered, too, that Mr. James Lewis and Mrs.
Gilbert had unimportant parts, and this tended not a
little to diminish the popu'arity of the piece. "The
Taming of the Shrew," on the other hand, has been
received with acclamation and enthusiasm; yet, in
my opinion, not at all more warmly than it deserved. It
is long since we have had in London such an all-round
satisfactory performance of a Shakspearean play;
and its general merit rises into exceptional excellence

in Miss Rehan's *Katharine*. I do not quite know what position Miss Rehan holds in America. It is clear that she is popular and highly esteemed, but I am not sure that your critics have claimed for her the rare and individual talent which we, on this side, are more and more inclined to accord to her. If her training is not quite perfect, she has temperament and inspiration; and (priceless gift in these days!) she can speak blank verse as if she felt its beauty. In academic elocution I should suppose her unskilled, but she needs it no more than a nightingale needs a course of singing lessons. Her performance of *Katharine*, in short, if not a great achievement in the highest walk of art, is, on its own level, perfect and incomparable. For my part, I can say with all sincerity, that the season 1887-88 will ever be marked in my memory by two delightful pictures, indelibly imprinted; the pictures of two American actresses in two Shaksperian characters: Miss Anderson as *Perdita*, and Miss Rehan as *Katharine*.

Dramatizations of American novels, too, have been very much to the fore. I have already spoken of "Mr. Barnes of New York," the least important of the list. An adaptation of Mr. Hodgson-Burnett's "Editha's Burglar" was produced at the Princess's without attracting much attention. Very different was the fate in store for "Little Lord Fauntleroy," which has actually been the occasion of a partial reform in our law of stage rights. A certain Mr. S. V. Seebohm bethought himself to dramatize Mrs. Burnett's charming story, and, having stolen the steed, requested Mrs. Burnett's permission to open the stable-door. Approached in this cavalier fashion, she naturally protested, and threatened an appeal to the law. Mr. Seebohm, unabashed, assured her that she had no legal rights whatever, and proceeded to produce his (?) play at an afternoon performance at the Prince of Wales's Theatre. Miss Annie Hughes, a young lady of much talent, played the little American Grandison excellently in every respect, except that she made him a big American Grandison. If, by taking thought, she could have reduced her stature by a cubit or so, she would have been perfect. The piece was successful, and was repeated every afternoon for some weeks, Mr. Seebohm meanwhile protesting loudly that he was but little indebted to Mrs. Burnett's book, and in fact that it had rather hampered his creative imagination. But Mrs. Burnett was not so easily disposed of. She hurried on her own adaptation of her story, arranged for its production at Terry's Theatre, secured Miss Vera Beringer, a little girl of the most remarkable talent, for the part of the hero, and had her trained by no less skilled an instructess than Mrs. Kendal. Her English publishers in the meantime proceeded against Mr. Seebohm. They did not contest his right to dramatize the book, but they argued that in multiplying copies of large and essential portions of it, he infringed their copyright. Rather to the surprise of many people (for it seemed that this simple remedy for a glaring abuse must have been thought of long ago), the case went in their favour, and Mr. Seebohm was ordered to deliver up within a certain time all copies of his play. The pirate of course promptly struck his flag, and his collapse was immediately followed by the triumphant production at Terry's Theatre of "The Real Little Lord Fauntleroy," which has since then been performed every afternoon. Little Miss Beringer, who is the daughter of a well-known pianist, plays the little Lord quite as cleverly as her predecessor, Miss Hughes, and looks the part infinitely better. It is one of those performances at which one scarcely knows whether to laugh or weep. I need hardly point out that the Fauntleroy Case, thus happily decided, has nothing to do with international copyright. Mrs. Burnett's position in the matter was precisely that of any English novelist whose work is adapted without his consent. As the law now stands, you are free to dramatize any novel you please, but you must not put your dramatization in writing. Even a single prompt-copy, containing any passage from the novel, or a colorable imitation of any passage, is an infringement of copyright. In short, the pirate may have his pound of flesh, but let him not, at his peril, shed one drop of Christian blood!—a highly satisfactory conclusion.

Another American novel, even more famous than "Little Lord Fauntleroy," has been twice dramatized this season. Two different versions of Hawthorne's "Scarlet Letter" were produced on two consecutive days, the one at the Royalty, the other at an Olympic matinée. The Royalty version, by the Hon. Stephen Coleridge and Mr. Norman Forbes, was by far the better of the two. It was brief, crisp, and interesting; but the last act, unfortunately, ended in a piece of strangely misplaced ingenuity. Roger

Chillingworth was publicly accused of being the author of Hester Prynne's shame : he in turn accused Dimmesdale ; whereupon the infuriated po, ulace, believing their beloved pastor maligned, fell upon the slanderer and lynched him ! Thus Dimmesdale was suffered to survive in the odour of undiminished sanctity, whilst Chillingworth was put to death as the seducer of his own wife ! This grotesquely perverted end utterly spoiled the play, and not even the fine acting of Miss Eleanor Calhoun as Hester Prynne could retrieve its fortunes. The other adaptation by Messrs. Charrington and Nelson was altogether maladroit and tedious.

The past season has seen the dissolution of two memorable managerial partnerships, and the promotion of two well known actors to managerial rank. Of the Clayton-Cecil management I shall speak later. The Hare-Kendal management at the St. James's has been even more important. It began in the autumn of 1879, and has thus lasted nine years. It has added only four original plays, indeed, to English dramatic literature—" The Falcon," by Lord Tennyson, and " The Moneyspinner," " The Squire," and " The Hobby-Horse," by Mr. A. W. Pinero ; but every production at the St. James's, whether original, revived, or adapted, was full of interest. Mr. and Mrs. Kendal and Mr. Hare, themselves the leading actors of our stage in their respective lines, always gathered about them an excellent company, and mounted their plays with singular liberality and taste. Their last season of management has been entirely devoted to revivals—" Lady Clancarty," " A

Scrap of Paper," Lovell's old play, "The Wife's Secret" (a disastrous failure), "The Ironmaster," and last of all "The Squire," which renewed the success of its first production. Mr. Hare, I understand, intends to go into management on his own account, while the Kendals' plans for the future are still unsettled. The two actors who have undertaken managerial responsibilities are Mr. Edward Terry, at his own new theatre in the Strand, and Mr. Beerbohm Tree at the Haymarket. Mr. Terry, after reviving two or three trivial farces, produced a three-act comedy by Mr. Pinero, entitled ' Sweet Lavender,"—an unpretentious and altogether delightful blending of quaint humour and honest sentiment. I am told that Mr. Pinero's plays are but little esteemed in America. They no doubt lose a great deal of their effect for lack of his careful and masterly stage-management; but otherwise I am at a loss to understand why his inexhaustibility and inventive humour should not appeal to you as much as to us. To my mind he is the master of our contemporary stage, the only writer (Mr. Gilbert, perhaps, excepted) whose work shows intellectual grip and originality, combined with thorough literary craftsmanship.

Mr. Beerbohm-Tree, at the Haymarket, seems to be the right man in the right place. He has certainly reconquered for the theatre the vogue which it lost under the disastrous management of the Bancrofts' successors, Messrs. Russell and Bashford. He opened his campaign with "The Red Lamp" (which had been produced at another theatre in the previous spring), and an adaptation of " Gringoire," by Messrs.

Walter Besant and W. H. Pollock, entitled "The Ballad-Monger." His own performance of the old police-spy *Demetrius*, in "The Red Lamp," is a masterpiece of character-acting, and the part of the *Princess Claudia Morakoff* enabled Mrs. Beerbohm-Tree to step into a far higher place among emotional actresses than she had hitherto attained. Mr. Robert Buchanan's "Partners," founded upon Daudet's "Fromont jeune et Risler aîné," was the new manager's next production. Here again Mr. Tree found opportunity for a striking character-creation in *Borgfeldt*, the counterpart of Daudet's *Risler;* and though the weakness of the last act seriously injured its effect, the play was, on the whole, successful. A more ambitious effort followed, in the shape of an adaptation by Messrs. W. G. Wills and Sydney Grundy of Brackvogel's "Narciss," introduced to the English public twenty years ago by Herr Bandmann. The new adaptation, entitled "The Pompadour," was very expensively mounted, Mrs. Tree taking the title-part, while her husband appeared as *Narcisse Rameau*, and Mr. Brookfield as *Voltaire*. The adapters, unfortunately, had taken extraordinary liberties, not only with history, but with common-sense. In their hands the *Narcisse Rameau* of Diderot's dialogue had become a sentimental and utterly inconceivable madman, while *Voltaire*, *Diderot*, and *Grimm* were made to wander through the Court of Versailles cracking the rudest and most antiquated jokes at each other's expense in a positively puerile fashion. The acme of absurdity was reached in the last act, when *Narcisse*, recognizing in the *Pompadour* his

D

own faithless wife, hurled at her a prophetic harangue, in which he proclaimed himself to be an embodiment of "THE REVOLUTION!!"—in 1764! "The Pompadour" was almost universally condemned; yet so entirely had Mr. Tree restored the vogue of the Haymarket, that people were curious to see the piece, in spite of the critics, and it continued for many weeks to draw tolerable houses. In the position he now occupies, Mr. Beerbohm-Tree has it in his power to do much, very much, for the welfare of the English stage. May he escape the pitfalls which beset the path of the actor-manager!

To the list of new managers I should perhaps add a manageress—Mrs. Bernard Beere; but her tenancy of the Opera Comique, though so far successful, is not likely to be permanent. She has produced two vulgar and cynical, but not uninteresting, plays, depicting English manners from the point of view of the third-rate society journalist. They were both adaptations of novels—Mr. F. C. Phillips's "As in a Looking-Glass, and Mrs. Campbell Praed's "Bond of Wedlock," rechristened "Ariane." In the former, Mrs. Beere played a heartless adventuress, in the latter, a woman of fashion, married to a drunken and dissolute husband. Both plays were so steeped in cynicism and scoundrelism as to secure for the Opera Comique the nickname of the Depravity Theatre. Mr. Burnand's amusing parody of "Ariane," entitled "Airey Annie," was cleverly played by Mr. Edouin and Miss Atherton at the Strand Theatre, not fifty yards distant from the house where the original play was running. Mr. Sydney Grundy's very neat adap-

tation of Von Moser's "Harun al Raschid," entitled
"The Arabian Nights," revived the declining fortunes
of Mr. Hawtrey's management at the Globe, just as
his lease of that theatre was expiring. The farce
was transferred to the Comedy Theatre, where its
popularity is not yet exhausted. At the Vaudeville,
Mr. Buchanan's "Sophia" made way, after a long
run, for Mr. H. A. Jones's "Heart of Hearts," a piece
in my opinion unworthy of Mr. Jones's talent. It was
very warmly received at first, but had only a brief
career, and was replaced, after a short interregnum,
by Mr. Buchanan's comedy of "Joseph's Sweetheart,"
founded upon Fielding's "Joseph Andrews." Mr.
Buchanan, it would appear, keeps filtered Fielding
always on draught, and the Vaudeville public shows
an insatiable taste for the somewhat vapid beverage.
Mr. Toole has produced at his own theatre a three-
act farce by Mr. and Mrs. Herman Merivale, entitled
"The Don." It is something of an improvement on
its predecessor, "The Butler," but is a sad falling off
from Mr. Merivale's earlier "form," to which we owe
"All for Her" and "Forget Me Not." Mr. Irving,
returning from the American tour of which such
triumphant accounts have reached us, opened his
short season at the Lyceum with the sempiternal
"Faust." It was replaced, after a few weeks, by
"The Amber Heart," a "poetic fancy," by Mr. A. C.
Calmour, and a two act version of "Robert Macaire."
"The Amber Heart" is a piece of maudlin sentimentality reminding one of Mr. Gilbert's least successful blank-verse plays, but without any of the
literary faculty which never deserts Mr. Gilbert, even

at his worst. Mr. Irving does not appear in it, but Miss Terry finds, in the heroine, a character after her own heart, and plays it with infinite grace and feeling. The admirers of Mr. Irving's grim vein of comedy found much to entertain them in his *Robert Macaire*, though a hideous disfigurement of face in which he indulged in the first night excited some protest and was afterwards modified.

Revivals of " Pinafore," " The Pirates," and " The Mikado," have occupied the whole season at the Savoy, but have not proved very attractive. On the other hand, " Dorothy," by Messrs. Stephenson and Cellier, is approaching its seven-hundreth representation at the Prince of Wales's, while " The Old Guard," a comic opera adapted from the French, has been very successful at the Avenue Theatre. A clever burlesque, named " Miss Esmeralda," by Messrs. Frederick Leslie and H race Mills, occupied the autumn season at the Gaicty. The regular Gaiety Company (including Mr. Leslie, Miss Farren, and Miss Silvia Grey) returned from the provinces at Christmas, and produced a burlesque, named " Frankenstein," by Richard Henry, the theatre-name of two sporting journalists. On the first night it was voted dull and over-decorated, and received with a storm of disapproval. Subsequently, however, it was licked into better shape, and drew crowded houses, until the company departed, about Easter, on a tour to Australia. Mr. Augustus Harris's Drury Lane pantomime of " Puss in Boots " was almost incredibly gorgeous, but by no means lively. The public, however, has come to look for spectacle rather than sport at Christmas-tide, and the rivalry of a much more amusing pantomime of "Jack and the Beanstalk" at Covent Garden in no way diminished the triumphs of "Augustus Druriolanus," as this worthy successor of Elliston loves to be entitled.

The season of French plays at the Royalty was rendered delightful by two visits from the elder Coquelin, one in the autumn, the other in the spring. Besides appearing in many of the best-known characters of his older repertory—*Mascarille*, *Scapin*, *Figaro*, *Gringoire*, *Don Annibal* in "L'Aventurière," and *Destournelles* in "Mademoiselle de la Seiglière" —this admirable actor gave us an opportunity of studying some of his most recent creations at the Français, as well as a good many impersonations in which the Parisian public has not yet had an opportunity of seeing him. To the former class belong Feuillet's *Chamillac* and *Bréchanteau* in "Un Parisien," and *Chantelaur* in "Le Député de Bombignac;" to the latter belong *Don Césare de Bazan*, *Noel* in "La Joie fait Peur," *Vivien Lefort* in Paul Delair's "L'Aîné," and last, but not least interesting, Molière's *Tartuffe* and *Mathias* in "Le Juif Polonais." *Tartuffe* is a character on which M. Coquelin has theories of his own. He has long ago argued in print that the tragic and terrible *Tartuffe* is a mistake, and that Molière intended him to be a comic character, the dupe of the play. He even maintains that the classic type of hypocrisy is not a hypocrite, but a self-deceiver. I do not find, however, that his performance of *Tartuffe* throws much new light on the character. It is grotesquely rather than grimly powerful, but comic it can scarcely be called. The interest of his *Mathias* in " Le Juif Polonais " lay in the comparison, or rather contrast, between it and Mr. Irving's *Mathias* in " The Bells." M. Coquelin's is the realistic, Mr. Irving's the romantic, conception of the part ; and the romantic is incomparably the more effective of the two. Mr. Irving throws all his intensity into a study of remorse ; M. Coquelin denies that the peasant murderer felt any remorse at all, devotes all his skill to a study of callousness. Whichever conception may be the correct one, according to the author's intention and the laws of human nature, there is not the least doubt that callousness is less dramatically interesting than remorse. It was said of Macready that he was a "great metaphysical actor." If we take the epithet in the sense in which Shakspere uses it when he speaks of "fate and metaphysical aid," we may extend this eulogy to Mr. Irving. M. Coquelin, on the other hand, has scarcely a trace of the metaphysical in his splendid and versatile talent.

M. Coquelin's autumn season was very well attended, but when he returned in spring his attraction had somehow declined, and he often played to disgracefully thin houses. Towards the close of his engagement, however, he produced the latest Parisian success, MM. Mars and Bisson's farce " Les Surprises du Divorce," which filled the little Royalty to overflowing. In almost all his performances he was supported by his son, M. Jean Coquelin, a highly promising young actor.

Death has been busy in the ranks of " the profession" during the past season. Mr. Chippendale, the most delightful *Sir Peter Teazle*, *Sir Anthony Absolute*, and *Mr. Hardcastle* of our time, passed away at a very advanced age, having outlived his mental faculties by some years. His wife, though much younger than he, followed him within a very few weeks to the grave. Mr. Creswick, an estimable tragedian of the school of Phelps, and Mr. W. J. Hill, a rotund and rubicund low comedian of genuine and even inimitable talent in his line, have also made their final exit. Our greatest loss, however, is that of Mr. John Clayton, a distinguished actor and excellent manager, cut off, when as yet he had barely crossed the threshold of middle age. Mr. Clayton made his first striking success as a romantic actor in the part of *Hugh Trevor* in "All for Her." Subsequently, as his increasing stoutness rendered him less fitted for "costume" parts, he was in great request for what we may call man-of-the-world characters, such as the elder *Beauclerc* in "Diplomacy," which he played to perfection. The early years of his management, in partnership with Mr. Arthur Cecil, at the Court Theatre, were more interesting than productive, in a pecuniary sense. The managers relied too much on belated cup and-saucer comedy and sentimental adaptations from the French. At last they "struck oil" in Mr. Pinero's ingenious farces, "The Magistrate, "The Schoolmistress," and "Dandy Dick." It was said that Mr. Clayton degraded his talent in playing *Colonel Lukyn*, *Admiral Rankling* and *Dean Jedd*, but for my part I cannot see anything degrading in such admirable performances. The popularity of "Dandy Dick" was not exhausted when the lease of the Court Theatre expired, and Messrs. Clayton and Cecil dissolved partnership. Mr. Clayton transferred the play to Toole's Theatre, while he hurried on arrangements for the building of a new Court Theatre (the old one having been pulled down) in the neighbourhood of Sloane Square. "Sepulcri immemor struis domos;" before the theatre was well begun the manager's career was ended. He died, almost suddenly, in Liverpool, leaving a widow (daughter of Mr. Dion Boucicault) and several young children.

The new Court Theatre, which is to be opened in September by Mrs. John Wood, is only one of several playhouses soon to be added to the active list. In Shaftesbury Avenue, the new street connecting Piccadilly Circus with New Oxford Street, at least three theatres are to be erected, two being already well advanced. One of these is the Lyric Theatre, which Mr. H. J. Leslie, is constructing out of the proceeds of "Dorothy;" the other is the Shaftesbury Theatre, built by Mr. John Lancaster for his wife, Miss Wallis, a Shaksperian actress of great provincial reputation. Mr. W. S. Gilbert, too, has secured a site in the neighbourhood of Trafalgar Square, on which he proposes to erect a theatre, to be called "The Garrick," with sundry structural and mechanical improvements of his own devising. Mr. Hare, according to present arrangements, will be the first lessee of the Garrick Theatre, and Miss Julia Neilson will be a leading member of the company. Miss Neilson is a young lady of striking physical gifts, who has recently decided, by Mr. Gilbert's advice, to abandon the career of a singer for that of an actress. She made her first appearance on any stage shortly before Easter, when she played *Cynisca* to Miss Mary Anderson's *Galatea* at a Lyceum matinée. Her success was remarkable, and she has since appeared at the Savoy Theatre in one or two other characters in Mr. Gilbert's blank-verse plays. Until the Garrick Theatre opens she will probably join the company with which Mr. Rutland Barrington intends to open the St. James's Theatre, early next autumn.

WILLIAM ARCHER.

1st July, 1888.

SCENIC ART IN MR. IRVING'S "FAUST."

A consideration of Mr. Henry Irving's production of
"Faust," naturally divides itself into two parts, pertaining respectively to the dramatic and to the spectacular side of the work.   At first these divisions
seem to be sharply defined in their individuality, and
to be distinctly differentiated, one from the other ;
indeed upon an initial hearing of the play the average
person is apt to find his attention involuntarily
absorbed by the one feature almost to the exclusion
of contemplation of the other.   This impression,
however, wears away upon a second or third hearing
and seeing of the work, and it is then clearly apparent
that these two features of the presentation are essentially and consistently interdependent, and that they
blend harmoniously, each adding to and enforcing the
effect of the other,   the combination resulting in a
homogeneous whole, well-balanced, artistic and of
distinct power.   In this, it seems plain enough, is the
great triumph of Mr. Irving, not alone as a stage
manager, but equally as a dramatic artist.   He has
made his stage settings not merely so much background for a spoken and acted tragedy, but a com-
ponent and very essential part of the tragedy itself.
They are not the frame for the picture ; they actually

belong to the picture, and it is in this respect that they differ most conspicuously from the stage work of their kind that we generally see. Hence it is that when "Faust" has been studied from the purely dramatic side there yet remains the consideration of it as a spectacle before one can fully comprehend and appreciate the perfection of the presentation as a whole.

Possibly the careless observer may have felt a certain disappointment on the first seeing of this play, since the production has been heralded and lauded as one of the most wonderful stage settings of this generation. This is not at all surprising, for we have come to associate the idea of magnificence in stage appointments with an abundance of tinsel, silks and satins, gorgeous trappings and an exuberance and a brilliancy in effects of colour and light that may rightly be, as they for the most part are, described as dazzling. To be sure the American stage has had its effective and artistic settings, notably perhaps those pertaining to several of Mr. Augustin Daly's productions ; but these, despite their admirable character generally, have not been able to influence popular taste seriously or to eradicate the deep-seated confidence of the public that the more gorgeous and bizarre the stage appears, the more worthy of admiration it is. This vitiated taste every production that aims at artistic excellence on this side of its presentation must contend with before it can secure recognition. Now Mr. Irving's "Faust" makes no concession to this Philistinism. It has been planned upon an entirely different basis, and the "Black Crook" quality of spectacle is agreeably absent from it. It does not essay in its stage effects to dazzle the eye; it appeals to the intellect and to the finer artistic sense. It is not as though you were listening to the brazen blare of trumpets; rather as you look you hear the passionate throbbing of the strings, the rich, mellow tones of the wood-wind. It follows then that appreciation of such a work of art cannot come from the mere sensual sensation of the moment; it is of deeper import, of more serious quality, and of more profound intellectual origin.

From a purely art point of view the quality that first app als for recognition in these settings is their truthful realism. The views of Nürnberg are exceptionally impressive in this particular of truth to their originals. First of all, as regards the science of the stage-carpenter, they are in a very wholesome manner unconventional in arrangement. You do not see the usual mechanical wings and flat back drop. In the St. Lorenz-Platz, and the church scenes, the square in front of the church is broken into by buildings; real streets lead out of it; the perspective is effectively managed, so that the eye is led away gradually into the distance, and is not brought up sharply against the back drop. The work of the artist is further seen in admirable touch in the treatment of the exteriors of the buildings. The colour, dark and low-toned, is remarkably rich and forceful, the carved work on the cathedral front is painted as an artist would paint it in a picture, and the statues are modelled in strong relief.

Here we have the quaint mediæval architecture, the

deep, age-toned colour of the stone buildings, and the dull, quiet atmosphere pervading all. You feel almost as though you were actually peering down upon the old square from a window in some one of the houses that border it, and the scene seems like a real bit taken out of the old German city, and transported hither by the magic of Mephistopheles himself. The sets and drops are not alone successes of stage mechanics; they are admirable productions of the artist's brush. It may be frankly held that they have been painted with a full thought of their stage use, and that therefore in themselves alone they would be found lacking at some points purely as works of art. But in a broader sense of effectiveness they are wholly admirable. They are a forcible example of clever and artistic adaptation of means to an end, and a painter's canvas could not in its way make these subjects more vividly real than they here appear under the illuminating effects of stage representation.

What is true of the Nürnberg street scenes is equally true of the other sets. Some one has already said substantially that the set showing *Faust's* study is, in conception, in style, and in general treatment worthy the school of Dürer. The aptness of the comparison must be apparent to any art student. As a matter of truth, the flavour of mediæval German art pervades and dominates all these settings, which may well have been arranged, studied and painted under the influence and the inspiration of the old German painters.

The house interiors are admirably studied, and are painted with a faithful attention to details, and to the

general character of the originals that is not only
effective in itself, but adds to the picturesque interest
in the movement of the drama. The two garden
scenes are splendid examples of pictorial art. The
garden of *Margaret* in particular is a beautiful
picture, with its quaint and picturesque cottage, its
vine-covered wall, and the view of the city towers in
the background. The three landscape scenes are
good examples of strong artistic work. The trees
and mountains, and the city wall are simply drop
scenes in the flat. They have been treated broadly
and forcibly, and with an excellent feeling for atmo-
spheric effect. If put on canvas on a reduced scale,
they would make strong exhibition pictures. The
scene showing the summit of the Brocken is also
distinguished for an impressive grandeur of conception, a boldness of handling, and a profound
colour treatment that are in the highest degree effective.

But praiseworthy as these settings are, merely as
products of the painter's brush, the resources of Mr.
Irving's genius are scarcely indicated until we look
at the results of his stage mechanism in the production of wonderful *mise-en-scène*. It is doubtful if any
stage has ever seen anything quite equal to this in all
respects. We notice now that the stage arrangements
and the painting of the sets have been cleverly devised for the best display of the effects to which they
are the background. In fact, the more we look at it
the more we are inclined to view these scenes in their
entirety as studies in colour, carried out in the harmonious relations of the painted drops and wings,

the movements and the costumes of the personages
of the play, the arrangement and manipulation of
lights and the various mechanical devices : as such we
must accord them the palm for a superb effectiveness.

Nothing could be more impressive, as conveying a
full sense of the situation, than the colour scheme of
the Witches' Kitchen, unless, indeed, it should be
admitted that the summit of the Brocken surpasses
it in that respect. The dark, damp, underground
cave, a subdued brown in colour, the grey garments
of the old witch, worn and worm-eaten, and seemingly heavy with a dank grave-mould, the flashes of
red light from the bubbling cauldron, from the lamps
that form the circle of incantation, and from the
nimbus in which *Mephistopheles* seems to move, make
a picture that is as grand in its well-balanced consistency as it is fascinating in its terrible weirdness.

The scene on the summit of the Brocken is not
more admirable, from a purely artistic point of view,
as relates to its colour scheme and its groupings ; but
it is conceived on a grander scale, and is more replete
with startling phenomena. The setting is of itself
sufficiently simple, only a world of broken cliffs and
rocks, with groups of withered trees. These have
been treated by the painter in cool greys, and the
effect of the whole is quiet and repressive than otherwise, although you feel at once the grandeur of the
scene. But when the act is fully on, witches fly
across the desolate space ; owls hoot and cry ; the
thunder rolls and the lightnings flash ; witches clad
in grey garments that cling to them like cerements

join in the hilarious revel; *Mephistopheles* in blood-red garb imperiously dominates the fearful throng from the summit of the crag, or joins in the dance, or sits on a rock fondling the ape children, while flashes of electric light gleam about him. Then the shower of fire beats down from the heavens upon the poor wretches grovelling at the feet of Satan, and the scene is brilliant with an infernal light.

It is easy to say that this is all theatrical display; is it not rather the exhibition of a tremendous dramatic force that is no less powerful in this dumb show than it would be in elaborate speech? But, passing over the grandeur of the conception, one secret of the effectiveness of this scene may be found in the artistic unity of the whole. It is but a single step from the sublime to the ridiculous, and one incongruous touch would turn into a farce what is now the sublimity of an infernal tragedy. Here again we are compelled to recognize a masterly colour treatment. The cold grey background of the landscape brings out most strongly the effect of the grey, unctuous tone of the witches' garments; and the *Mephistopheles* figure, the play of light and the fiery shower all harmonize perfectly, and make a series of ever-changing pictures that appeal to the eye with their purely æsthetic perfection as they appeal to the imagination in the thoughts suggested by them.

Naturally, the costuming of the people contributes much to the effect of the production on its spectacular side. The costumes bear evidence of having been carefully studied from or'ginals, and they give a pronounced and agreeable local colour to the scenes;

reference, of course, is now made to the scenes dealing with the mortals. This costuming is a decided feature of the presentation, and it reproduces for us very faithfully, with much picturesqueness and beauty, and with striking contrasts of colour, the life of the period.

Of scarcely less interest than the colour arrangements are the wonderful effects of light. This feature has been carefully studied, and shows much artistic feeling, as well as skill in the developing of situations and the creating of vivid impressions. For a great part of the time the stage is kept in a semi-darkness, and in and out of this the personages of the play seem to move, as though they came from the shades of another world or were enveloped in the cloud of tragedy that hangs over them. *Mephistopheles* brings with him the blood-red light of the infernal regions, and now and then a ghastly hue illumines his face, and sharply emphasizes the Satanic character of his leering features; a shifting play of ghostly light and shadow touches the gruesome figures in the Witches' Kitchen and on the Brocken summit; electric sparks flash from the sword of *Mephistopheles* in the duel scene; fire and vapour spring from the underground regions at the will of his Satanic majesty: these are some of the more remarkable effects in this direction. You may call this mechanical if you will, but it is all exceedingly clever and artistic, and in a wonderful manner it attains the supreme end of all stage representation—the intensifying of the impressiveness of the situation. In quieter mood, the sunset and moonlight effects and the studied arrangement of

E

lights in the death scene of Valentine are alike admirable for their naturalistic character. The apotheosis may also be cited to show how much has been secured by the careful application of the principles of light. Here we have the figures brought out with marvellous clearness and distinctness; in solidity of modelling they have all the value of a sculptor's creations.

Even at the risk of trenching upon the province of the dramatic critic, a reference to the actions of the people, so far as it relates to the pictorial features of the production, must not be omitted. The groupings and the movements of the people on the stage are tremendously vital, and give an air of reality to every scene. This, you are impelled to say, is life itself, not its mere counterfeit presentment. Just so must these men and women of old Nürnberg have conducted themselves. What indeed could be more delightful than the action of the woman clasping the frightened child to her breast in the Lorenz-Platz scene? It is a touch of genuine human nature, and yet that may be cited as only one example from among many that show the perfection of detail that characterizes the disposition and the management of the supernumeraries on the stage. The production in this particular is a constant succession of moving tableaux, splendidly spirited, artistic, and impressive. Every group makes a beautiful picture; the death scene of *Valentine*, for instance, in its picturesqueness of composition and its breadth and vigour of treatment, vividly suggests much of the power of Rembrandt's "Night Watch." Mr. Irving is constantly posing and moving about in a way to heighten the feeling that you are looking upon a picture of real life, and as for Miss Terry, she is a perfect poem of beauty in her graceful movements and her artistic poses. A painter might well go into rapture over her attitudes. Could anything be more agreeable to the eye, in its way, than the half-reclining position that she takes in the chair in her chamber when she discovers the jewels, or, indeed, a hundred other poses that are assumed with equal grace and charming *naïveté?* This "Faust," admirable as it is, would lose much were this picturesque and beautiful figure taken from it.

LYMAN H. WEEKS.

PART II.

THE LAST YEAR OF WALLACK'S.

THE most noteworthy fact in relation to the season of 1887-88 at Wallack's Theatre was the statement, made public several months ago, that there would be no stock company at this theatre after May 5th of the present year. It is well understood that Mr. Henry E. Abbey, a very able and experienced manager after his fashion, succeeded Mr. Wallack as director of our most famous playhouse last autumn. Mr. Wallack, who had been disabled by sickness, then retired from active service, and Mr. Abbey attempted to take his place. Mr. Abbey is remarkably clever at handling a travelling company, with some "star," like Mr. Irving, Miss Anderson or Madame Bernhardt, at the head of it; but he discovered within a brief period that he could not handle a company like the one attached to Wallack's Theatre. His poor fortune discouraged him finally, and he was induced to announce the "last weeks of the Wallack company." Mr. Wallack was, thereupon, called back to the theatre, and the final performances given by this stock company enjoyed the benefit of his dexterous supervision.

The season of 1887-88 was, in consequence, the closing season of Wallack's Theatre; for, although the house will continue to be known as Wallack's, its peculiar distinction and its tradition will remain only as a part of stage history. Whether the two chief members of the Wallack company, Mr. Wallack himself and Mr. John Gilbert, will be seen again on the stage, cannot be answered with anything like assurance. I have received personal declaration, however, from both Mr. Gilbert and Mr. Wallack, that neither has the slightest intention of retiring yet from the stage. Mr. Gilbert is in sound health and prime spirits; he was never a better actor than he is to-day; it seems unreasonable that he should be expected to relinquish a work to which he has devoted so large a portion of his honourable life. As to Mr. Wallack, his acting was still buoyant and bright three or four years ago, and if his crippled leg were once strong and limber again, he might be counted upon to make a brilliant exit from the theatre. Nevertheless, and in spite of the natural desire of both actors to show themselves once more, there is a possibility that the end of the Wallack company means the end of their public career. No one hopes more earnestly than the present writer that such shall not be the case.

I need not remind the reader that there have been three Wallack's Theatres, nor that the third has been less like the Wallack's of mellow record than either of its predecessors. The charm of Wallack's, at its best, lay in harmonious adjustment of players; in the understanding and sympathy which those players brought to the performance of comedy, especially "old comedy;" in suave methods, which were an in-

heritance rather than an independent creation. At the
third Wallack's Theatre there was always lacking
something of the manner, something of the taste and
feeling, which we had associated with the name of
Wallack. The company was unbalanced, composed
of elements that jarred against one another. Mr.
Osmund Tearle, and various excellent actors whom
I might name, seemed curbed, while they occupied
places in the Wallack company, to unnatural sub-
duedness. There was a perceptible conflict between
their methods and the Wallack methods. Even Miss
Rose Coghlan lacked precisely those qualities which
made Miss Ada Dyas and other " leading ladies " of
Wallack's so interesting when observed from the
Wallack standpoint. There were few performances
of old comedy given at this theatre last season, few
performances of any sort of genuine comedy, that
were not a trifle tiresome ; they seemed to be perfunctory copies of the things we used to admire with
rare zest. If public taste, therefore, for old comedy
has appeared to decline, if Wallack's Theatre has got
into a state of decadence, it is partially, without
doubt, because most of the actors of the Wallack
school had passed away. The public may have
wanted the old meat, but they wanted the old sauce
too.

Outside of the fact that the final season of the Wallack company meant disintegration, there was little to
bring it into prominence. With Mr. Wallack absent
from the home and the company ; with a company
that was not homogeneous, without special policy or
ambition, the theatre had slight chance of rising

much beyond conventionality. As a matter of truth the season was not particularly interesting. Mr. Abbey introduced his bright and pretty wife as a conspicuous member of the company at the beginning of the season ; but Mrs. Abbey was not at home, so to speak in the company. I have seen her in characters to which she gave a certain grace and finesse. On the Wallack stage she performed characters with which she must have had the smallest amount of sympathy. Her retirement, long before the season came to an end, was, perhaps, a matter of course.

The season opened on the evening of October 11th, 1887. The play was "The Mouse Trap," by Sydney Grundy. Mr. Osmund Tearle appeared as *Lord Normantower*, Mr. Charles Groves as *Sir Peter Lund*, Mr. E. D. Ward as *Philip Selwyn*, Mr. S. Sothern as *Tom Vainder*, Mrs. Abbey as *Beatrice Selwyn* Miss Coghlan as *Kate Derwent*, and Miss Enid Leslie as *Mildred Selwyn*. "The Mouse Trap" told a trivial and impossible story in a curiously disconnected manner. It was a poor piece, though in part cleverly written. Mr. Grundy has frequently demonstrated his skill in dialogue, but he appears to lack, what nearly all contemporary English dramatists lack, the ability to put together a probable, novel, and interesting narrative. In "The Mouse Trap," a woman jilts her lover for no conceivable reason, and, for as little reason, attempts to poison her husband. Her acts are meant to be impressive, whereas, in fact, they are merely grotesque.

The prompt failure of Mr. Grundy's play astonished Mr. Abbey, who was compelled to fall back at once

upon a revival. "Caste" was revived on October
24th, with Miss Coghlan as *Esther*, Mrs. Abbey as
Polly, Mr. Tearle as *George D'Alroy*, Mr. Charles
Groves as *Eccles*, Mr. E. D. Ward as *Captain Haw-
tree*, Mr. T. W. Robertson as *Sam Gerridge*, and
Madame Ponisi as the *Marquise*. This was, to say
the least, an awkward distribution of parts. Miss
Coghlan's fine and clearly circumscribed talent slum-
bered in the character of *Esther*. Mrs. Abbey was an
extremely artificial *Polly*. As to Mr. Tearle, he was
certainly not meant by nature to shine in a Robert-
sonian play; his *D'Alroy* was lumpishly unromantic.
Mr. Groves—a comedian of real humour—was an
amusing *Eccles*, and Mr. Robertson played *Gerridge*
with snap and intelligence. Mr. Robertson, by the
way, had been "imported" to manage the Wallack
stage, and his ideas were not always those which
Wallack audiences had taken to their hearts. Some
of the most winning episodes that Mr. Wallack had
introduced into "Caste" and "School" were ruth-
lessly cut out by Mr. Robertson;—and these plays
were not improved under such aggressive British
treatment. A revival of "School" followed "Caste"
on November 15th, with a painfully unprofitable
result. What had previously seemed fresh, droll or
even fascinating in this gossamer little piece, took on
now the appearance of stupidity. When "School,"
after a forced run of two weeks, was replaced by
"Forget-me-not," there was a general sign of relief.
"Forget-me-not" had been done many times in New
York, and it was one of the very successful plays
produced at the second Wallack's Theatre. Miss

Coghlan's *Stephanie* has been justly admired for its
brilliant colouring, its feline smoothness and its cool
equipoise.   But it must be confessed that Mr. Abbey's
luck was not greatly enhanced by this revival.   The
theatre which he had undertaken to conduct continued to be a steady drain upon his purse.   Failure
dogged him again when, on the evening of December
28th, he produced Madame Selina Dolaro's play, " In
the Fashion," which had been given previously one
afternoon at the Madison Square Theatre.   Mr.
Tearle, Mr. Eben Plympton, Mr. Edwards, Miss
Coghlan, and Mrs. Abbey had parts in Madame
Dolaro's play, and the acting was, therefore, uni-
formly good.   But the radical extravagances of the
piece were not relished by our public, and, in spite of
some rather effective situations and many bright bits
of talk, " In the Fashion " was speedily removed
from the stage.

Up to this period—January 20th, 1888—Mr. Abbey
had brought forward two new plays, and revived
three old ones; the theatre had been seldom filled,
and its prospects gloomy.   Yet Mr. Abbey was
courageous enough to produce a play like " L'Abbé
Constántin," of delicate fabric, and not too well
suited to our stage.   His courage, however, was
creditable to him ; for " L'Abbé Constántin," barring
its strain of unnatural sentimentality, is a wholesome
and honest piece.   In Paris, as every one knows, it
has been received cordially and praised with un-
wonted fervour ; that is because the French recognize themselves in " L'Abbe Constántin," and we
Americans can hardly be expected to do that.   As

a picture of simple provincial life in France, "L'Abbé Constántin" has serious value; and a dreamy haze of romance surrounds this picture. But the permanent charm of the play must be sought in the quaintly pathetic character of the old Abbé, a character acted by Mr. Gilbert with rare sweetness and truth. Mr. Clinton Stuart made the American adaptation of the "L'Abbé Constántin," and, although his work showed good taste and discretion, he might have used his pen with greater boldness. Mrs. Abbey bade farewell to the stage in "L'Abbé Constántin," which failed to attain sufficient popularity to encourage Mr. Abbey in further experiment. On the contrary, he had now made up his mind that the Wallack company was nothing more nor less than a drag upon him, and he proposed to get rid of it. The public read in the newspapers one morning that the Wallack actors would give their last performances in a series of old comedy revivals, and that at the close of the season the company would be disbanded. The announcement came like a shock to us, for we had grown to look upon the company as an essential portion of our social life. But no one was surprised, for what happened had seemed inevitable.

"London Assurance" was revived on February 20th, and was followed by "Old Heads and Young Hearts," "Town and Country," "Money," "She Stoops to Conquer," and "The School for Scandal." In these plays, Mr. Tearle was intrusted with the parts that had been performed with inimitable grace and airiness in days past by Mr. Wallack. If Mr. Tearle could have brought to his acting of such parts some really thoughtful appreciation of them, he might have been accepted as a passable substitute for Mr. Wallack ; but his heavy style and sluggish nature were as strangely unsuited to the gay creatures of artificial comedy as they were to the translucent simplicity of Robertson. There was considerable vigour—a hearty animal spirit—in his performance of Charles Surface, it is true, and he carried that character with moderate success. But in "Money," and "She Stoops to Conquer," he was more than distasteful. "Town and Country" was the dreariest of all these revivals, and, candidly, it is not a good play because it is an old one ; it gave Mr. Gilbert a chance, however, to depict a character which had been well-nigh lost to the stage. Mr. Gilbert, indeed, was the stately presence that lent dignity and interest to the revivals, and it seemed proper enough that this should be so ; for around Mr. Gilbert's form and name are clustered the rich traditions of Wallack's Theatre. Two of his associates, who were also seen with keen pleasure in the old comedies, were Madame Ponisi and Henry Edwards, both sterling players, both representatives of a school which is fast disappearing. The performances of the "School for Scandal" were, on the whole, more satisfactory than any of the others. As I have already said, Mr. Tearle was a spirited *Charles*, Miss Coghlan was a delightful *Lady Teazle*, and who can ever forget the ripe method, the old-fashioned courtesy, the absolute sincerity, of John Gilbert's *Sir Peter* ? I should add, too, that there is probably no better *Sir Oliver* on our stage than Mr. Edwards.

So much for the record of the last season of our favourite Wallack company. It was not a season that we shall look back to with much complacency, although Mr. Abbey must not be blamed too severely for having failed where most others would unquestionably have failed. The future of the theatre, in his hands, is assured, because he will be hereafter on safe ground.

GEORGE EDGAR MONTGOMERY.

THE WALLACK TESTIMONIAL.

[MONDAY EVENING, MAY 21st, 1888.]

THE Wallack testimonial performance of "Hamlet," was given in the Metropolitan Opera-house, New York, and was carried to a conclusion with scarcely a single slip or accident, amid such continual manifestations of sympathy, pleasure, and enthusiasm as must have gratified the highest ambitions of its promoters.

There is no doubt that the tribute to Mr. Wallack would have taken on a yet more thoroughly popular character than it did if the construction of the house had permitted a larger invasion of those classes who on occasions of this sort are compelled to avail themselves of what is known as the "general admission." The amount of standing-room in the Metropolitan Opera-house is extremely small, and every inch of it was packed to suffocation before the doors had been open for more than five minutes. The holders of tickets who were not in the first rush had the right of remaining within the limits of the building, but they might just as well have been in Central Park, so far as seeing or hearing anything that was happening on the stage was concerned. The solid blocks of humanity wedged in the few narrow spaces alloted to them presented a strange contrast to the general

emptiness which prevailed for some time in other
parts of the great interior. But the first comers were
not condemned to any long period of loneliness. It
had been announced repeatedly that the performance
would begin punctually, and after half-past seven
o'clock the seats began to fill rapidly in all directions,
and when Mr. Walter Damrosch raised his baton for
the beginning of the overture, there was scarcely a
vacant place to be seen anywhere. A list of the
prominent persons who were present would occupy
more space than can be afforded, and any mere selection would be invidious. In whatever direction the
eye turned, it fell upon a face well known in some
line of public, social, literary, or artistic life. The
heaviest military gun was General Sherman, in beaming
good-humour—a perfect illustration of grim-visaged
war smoothing his wrinkled front—and the brightest
political light was Mayor Hewitt, divested of all his
official terrors. Club life had its representatives
everywhere, and the mercantile and legal fraternities
contributed some of their sturdiest pillars. Among
these bulwarks of society might be seen here and
there less reputable persons, whose faces are never
absent from any great gathering of this kind; a
few fast men about town and two or three lawyers,
more notorious than famous, cheek by jowl with
some of the greatest dignitaries of the bench. It
was manifestly a cosmopolitan celebration, consti-
tuting the most eloquent of tributes to an actor. Age
and wealth and learning combined to give it solidity
and emphasis, youth filled it with ardour, beauty
endowed it with brightness and splendour, and

flowers lightened a somewhat heavy air with colour and fragrance. The scenes before and behind the curtain rivalled each other in interest, and the heart of Mr. Wallack must have swelled with thoroughly honest and grateful pride when he reflected that they were created for his special honour. Seldom, indeed, has any artistic life been crowned with so splendid a triumph as this.

The kindly and generous motive which was the source of this remarkable tribute to one of the most striking figures in the theatrical guild would exempt it naturally and properly from deliberate criticism, but the performance as a whole was so good, so entirely worthy of its object, that there is no polite necessity for taking refuge in insincere and meaningless generalities. The inevitable lack of rehearsal was apparent, of course, more than once, but not often ; and the general result afforded indisputable proof of the abundance of excellent material upon the New York stage for the interpretation of the noblest masterpieces of the poetic drama, when organized by intelligent direction, and demonstrated, moreover, the keen appreciation of the public for what is best and most elevating in theatrical art. To many, possibly even a majority of the audience, owing to the bad acoustic qualities of the house, a great part of the performance must have been little better than a dumb-show, but the picturesqueness and vitality of the action, aided by the familiarity of the story, sufficed to rivet the attention of the spectators from first to last. It would be tedious to dwell in detail upon all the minor features of the production,

and particular reference will be made, therefore, only
to those performers who especially distinguished
themselves. Mr. Booth has not been seen to such
advantage in *Hamlet* for many years. He seemed to
be inspired by the occasion, and acted with all his
wonted subtlety and precision, and with much more
than his wonted fire and spirit. His delivery was
marked by extraordinary delicacy of shading and
emphasis, and his facial expression was as varied and
significant as ever. His work was masterly throughout, and evoked repeated outbursts of applause. Mr.
Barrett, too, honestly won the plaudits bestowed upon
him for his impersonation of the *Ghost*, which he
enacted with fine solemnity and most welcome re-
straint. The *Polonius* of Mr. Gilbert, it is needless to
say, was admirable ; in no sense deficient in humour,
but without a trace of buffoonery, slow in wit and
portentous in speech, but venerable withal, and shrewd
within certain limitations. The *Laertes* of Mr.
Plympton was another admirable bit of work, full of
genuine passion and feeling, but rather wild of aspect.
Mr. Joseph Wheelock won a hearty round of applause
by his spirited declamation of the lines allotted to the
First Actor, and Rose Coghlan endowed the *Player
Queen* with a regal presence and some semblance of
emotion. The *Ophelia* of Modjeska was a delightful
addition to her studies of Shaksperian women, and
distinctly original. Her mad scenes were exceedingly pathetic, and wonderful in their variety. Her
love for *Hamlet* in the early scenes is marked very
strongly, and her conception of the character is
generally stronger and more abounding in contrasts

than that adopted by most actresses. The personality in her hands acquires greater tragic significance, without losing anything in the way of gentleness or charm. In grace, it is almost needless to add, it is superlative. One of the great hits of the evening was the *Grave-Digger* of Mr. Jefferson, which was delightful in its quaint humour and its exquisite naturalness. Wm. J. Florence, as the second *Grave-Digger*, had very little to do, but did that little well. The *King* of Mr. Mayo was not a very successful effort, but Miss Gertrude Kellogg was a thoroughly satisfactory *Queen*. The other characters were all well filled, but do not require individual mention.

The event of the evening was the appearance of Mr. Wallack, who came forward after the second act, and was greeted with a storm of applause, which was continued for many minutes. When silence was restored, he delivered his speech, with many skilful touches of humour and sentiment, and many familiar reflections of his most admired stage manner.

Almost every word was received with applause, especially the words which hinted at the possibility of his return to the stage. Everybody was pleased to see him apparently so vigorous, and seconded his hope that his obstinate leg, which alone keeps him from the stage, may be cured before long. He was the chief speaker of the evening, for although Mr. Booth, Mr. Barrett, Mr. Jefferson, and Mr. Florence were all called before the curtain, they declined to speak. When the curtain had fallen for the last time, although it was then after midnight, the people still clamoured for more speeches, and would not be satisfied until Mr. Palmer stepped forward and announced that Mr. Wallack had gone home. Mr. Palmer also said that last evening was the happiest of his life, and he and Mr. Daly are certainly entitled to all the congratulation showered upon them, for they have conducted a most difficult enterprise to a most brilliant termination. When he retired, the audience too went home and the Opera-house was soon emptied. Thus ended an evening which will live long in the memories of all who participated in the celebration, and above all in the heart of Mr. Wallack.

As a matter of record, the full cast is appended :—

Hamlet	Edwin Booth
Ghost of Hamlet's Father	Lawrence Barrett
King Claudius	Frank Mayo
Polonius	John Gilbert
Laertes	Eben Plympton
Horatio	John A. Lane
Rosencranz	Charles Hanford
Guildenstern	Lawrence Hanley
Osric	Charles Koehler
Marcellus	Edwin H. Vanderfelt
Bernardo	Herbert Kelcey
Francisco	Frank Mordaunt
First Actor	Joseph Wheelock
Second Actor	Milnes Levick
First Grave-Digger	Joseph Jefferson
Second Grave-Digger	W. J. Florence
Priest	Harry Edwards
Ophelia	Helena Modjeska
The Queen	Gertrude Kellogg
The Player Queen	Rose Coghlan

J RANKEN TOWSE.

MR. PALMER'S PRODUCTIONS.

[MADISON SQUARE THEATRE, 1887-88.]

THE Madison Square Theatre represents, above all,
a personality, and that personality is Mr. A. M.
Palmer. In other words, the Madison Square Theatre
is simply a continuation, so to speak, of the old
Union Square Theatre, a house once famous, and
famous through the skill, intelligence, and ability of
Mr. A. M. Palmer. What was observed most atten-
tively, enjoyed most keenly, at the Union Square
Theatre, when Mr. Palmer had charge of that place,
is again observed and enjoyed at the Madison Square
Theatre, of which he has now charge. He has not
repeated himself precisely in changing from one
theatre to the other; but he has stayed in ruts of
sound and honest method, and these are the conserva-
tisms that every theatrical manager should be glad
enough to stick to.

At the Union Square Theatre Mr. Palmer gave
thought chiefly to the contemporaneous French
Drama. There he produced some of the most interesting plays by Sardou, Feuillet. Dumas and other
popular writers of France. He produced also a few
English and American pieces. But he relied chiefly
upon the stage of Paris. When he succeeded the

Mallory brothers in the conduct of the Madison Square Theatre, it was supposed naturally that he would still look to French authors for his most serious work. But he has done nothing of the sort. He has branched out in many directions. He has sought plays from English, French, and American authors, without special predilection for a single nationality. In brief, he has modified a policy which seemed to belong to him at one period, and yet he has not modified his methods. As I have said already, what was enjoyed at the Union Square Theatre is enjoyed at the Madison Square Theatre. To put the fact sharply, his manner to-day is the manner of old. The charm which pervaded his presentation of "The Danicheffs" (one of the really beautiful and impressive performances that I have witnessed, perfect in treatment, perfect in acting) is the same charm that we have felt in the performance of "Jim the Penman" and of "Elaine," two plays as dramatically opposed in sentiment as two plays could possibly be.

The Madison Square Theatre, it should be stated, has offered a much too restricted scope to the energy and progressiveness of a manager like Mr. Palmer. The house is absurdly small, the stage a cramped little spot in which fine effects—strong dramatic illusions—cannot be attained. Big plays are not produced in miniature theatres, and there is no one to whom we look more eagerly than to Mr. Palmer for big plays. It is a pity, therefore, that he has had so much to do with miniature theatres.

Still, under his management, the Madison Square Theatre has offered much prosperous and brilliant entertainment. During the season which began last October and ended in the late spring of the present year, the record of this house was, to say the least for it, creditable. That season was not remarkable for productions of the best value, although it was in many respects very interesting. "Jim the Penman" was revived at its beginning, and was acted for six weeks. Sir Charles Young's striking play was followed by Mr. A. R. Cazauran's version of Dennery's "Martyre"—under title of "The Martyr"—on the evening of November 7th. "The Martyr" had the comparatively short run of four weeks. It was replaced by a dramatization of Lord Tennyson's "Elaine," made by George Parsons Lathrop and Henry Edwards, December 6th. "Elaine" ran six weeks. Then came "Heart of Hearts," by Henry Arthur Jones, with a run of eleven weeks. Robert Buchanan's "Partners" brought the season to a close; it was given its first representation on April 2nd, and was on the stage four weeks.

I may add that the special summer season at the Madison Square Theatre has a certain importance. The engagement of Mr. Richard Mansfield was, as usual, extremely popular, for Mr. Mansfield is an actor whose rare gifts of mind and talent are profoundly appreciated in New York; and Mr. Palmer is financially interested in that bright young actress, Miss Effie Elssler, who, at this moment of writing, may be seen in Mr. Clinton Stuart's clever and original arrangement of "Antoinette Rigeaud," which he calls "The Keepsake."

Of "Jim the Penman," which opened the season,

no fresh word can now be set down. "Jim the
Penman" is the one play by its author which has
succeeded, both here and in England, and of its class
it is generally held to be a particularly able, compact,
skilfully constructed, effective drama. It is a curious
illustration of novel method applied to a threadbare
theme. It aroused excited attention during the
season of 1886-87, and it was hardly less popular
when it was revived during the following season.
The performances of Mrs. Agnes Booth, Mr. H. M.
Pitt, and Mr. E. M. Holland in "Jim the Penman"
will long be remembered with peculiar pleasure.

Dennery's "Martyre" was hailed, at its first production in France, as a drama entirely worthy of the
author of "The Two Orphans." Several adaptations
of it were made for the American stage, one by Mr.
Clinton Stuart for Miss Clara Morris. Mr. Stuart's
arrangement was a rather close translation, and Miss
Morris gave in it another exhibition of her mono-
tonously crude—not to say unrefined—genius. As
to Mr. Cazauran's version of the same play, as presented at the Madison Square Theatre, that was
hardly less disagreeable than the original French
work, and perhaps a trifle more improbable. Every
situation in "The Martyr" was strained; reality was
replaced by hysterics; probability was sacrificed to
melodramatic trickery. The piece was gloomy, tearful, and overdone in all respects. One need hardly
be surprised, therefore, that it was rather frankly dis-
liked, in spite of occasional episodes marked by real
strength; moreover, Mrs. Booth was singularly
unfitted to her part, which she acted with utter frigi-

dity, and to which Miss Morris, at any rate, brought a highly nervous and emotional temperament.

"Elaine" was one of the charming experiments in which Mr. Palmer delights to indulge himself now and then. These experiments are apt to be costly, even while they show artistic honesty. One may recognize the truth at first blush, that a poem like "Elaine"—a sweet and candid study of young and passionate love—has no potent dramatic element in it. It was not meant for the intense cold light of the stage, but for the sympathetic imagination, communing with itself, possibly in a solitude of silence and stars. Yet it is satisfactory to record that "Elaine" on the stage brought tears to our eyes, moved our hearts, stirred our imaginations. Granting any criticism which could be put against such a translucently poetic piece intentionally, why should we object to having seen such a piece? I confess that the play, "Elaine,"—not to confound it with the poem—remains in my memory as a lovely recollection of the stage. Its exquisite and luminous pictures, its winning touches of tenderness and pathos, its flower-like fragility—all this seemed foreign to the theatre, and yet it was all beautiful in the theatre. I presume that Mr. Edwards may be credited with the construction of "Elaine" as a play, and he accomplished something of a feat against stern obstacles. As to Mr. Lathrop's text—composed in part of Lord Tennyson's verse and in part of his own—that was marvellously facile and equal. "Elaine" was very cleverly played, especially by Mr. Alexander Salvini as *Launcelot*, Miss Marie Burroughs as

Guinevere, and by two or three others ; the delicate expression given to the character of *Elaine* by Miss Annie Russell, however, seemed to be the result of spontaneous genius.

Of Mr. Jones's " Heart of Hearts " I have little to write in praise. This was unquestionably a weak play, founded upon a puerile motive, and trivial in its treatment. The story of the piece is simple to the extreme point of triteness : a rich young Englishman loves the niece of his butler—who is one of the most astoundingly unreal butlers that have served their time—and insists that his aristocratic mother shall receive his betrothed. A vagabond father of the girl steals a ruby—a family heirloom—known as the " heart of hearts," and this being found in the girl's possession, she is accused of theft. Her lover, and her uncle, the butler, however, believe in her innocence, and this is clearly proved after she has passed through a few absurd vicissitudes. The situations in " Heart of Hearts " are ancient and improbable, the pathos superficial, the humour decidedly coarse. This play gave pleasure to few persons, though it was well presented and fairly acted. In the cast were Miss Marie Burroughs, Mrs. E. L. Davenport, Mr. Louis Massen, Mr. E. M. Holland, and Mr. J. L. Stoddart.

It reems to be without question that Mr. Palmer looked to Mr. Buchanan's play, " Partners," as about the most serious production of his season. This play had been received with decided favour in London, and it was known to be based, in a measure, upon one of the famous novels of recent literature. Moreover, Mr. Buchanan is himself a writer of reputa-

tion—too prolific and versatile a writer for the highest
kind of reputation—yet a man of brilliant endowment.
Mr. Buchanan has succeeded rather well in building
a play, so to speak, out of one of Fielding's novels;
it was felt, when the announcement was made that
he had built one out of Daudet's "Fromont Jeune
et Risler Aîné," that he might be successful at this
second and not less hazardous venture. But I fancy,
on the whole, that those who are acquainted with
Mr. Buchanan's "Partners," prefer not to think of it
in association with such a potent and original book
as "Fromont Jeune et Risler Aîné."

The popularity of plays appears to depend measur-
ably upon the skilful manner in which they approach
the commonplace. The material which goes to
make what we often speak of as a strong play
would make a feeble novel. And the subtle distinction which lifts a novel into literature is quite as
often the thing we do not expect to find nor care to
find in a play. The beauty, the power, the courage
and character of Daudet's novel are not reproduced,
indeed, barely suggested, in Mr. Buchanan's "Partners." This piece is really a dexterous bit of
commonplace, a threadbare touching upon a great
theme, a feeble dallying with actual life. It is a good
illustration of the stage in its attitude towards society
and morals. The heroine—she who takes the part of
the living and imperishable *Sidonie*—is a silly wife of
the average kind, small-minded enough to be tempted,
not bold enough to commit herself to any positive
thought or action. The hero, on the other hand, is
a man of the most positive character. He is the

woman's husband ; a German of plebeian birth, *Henry Borgfeldt. Borgfeldt's* honesty, ingenuousness, manliness, and simple passion, are certainly worth all the rest of Mr. Buchanan's play. Yet there are minor characters that are neatly sketched, several taking situations, and at least one scene of really tragic interest.

Among those who had places in the cast of " Partners " were Mr. Alexander Salvini as *Borgfeldt*, Miss Marie Burroughs as *Claire*, Miss Mathilde Madison as *Mrs. Harkaway*, Mr. Walden Ramsay as *Charles Derwentwater*, Mr. C. P. Flockton as *Dickinson*, Miss May Robson as *Alice*, and Mr. E. M. Holland as *Algernon Bellair*—a very even and excellent distribution of characters.

One might believe that Mr. Buchanan had written " Partners "—shutting his eyes to all its improbabilities and conventionalities—for the single purpose of giving Mr. Salvini a rare opportunity to display copious natural talent. Mr. Salvini had, of course, revealed his talent previously. Even in " Elaine " he did some fine things ; though his acting in " Elaine " was, in the main, merely bearish. In a certain play, acted on a recent afternoon, at the Madison Square Theatre, his acting brought back to memory the glow and the strength—and much of the intelligence—of his father. In " Partners," however, he was called upon to perform what is technically described as a " character part," the part of a middle-aged German, brought up in a hard school of life, tender at heart, though rough in manner, gentle as a child or stern as a judge. Mr. Salvini treated this character with

absolute ease and sincerity, and by it he demonstrated both his versatility and his native genius.
But, then, he can be quite as uninteresting as he can
be interesting ; he may accept this hint for what it is
worth.   His future on the stage, it seems to me, is
assured.

GEORGE EDGAR MONTGOMERY.

"THE WIFE" AT THE LYCEUM.

THE first season of Mr. Daniel Frohman's new stock
company at the Lyceum Theatre, New York, proved
to be in every sense a most successful one. Beyond
this there is little to say of it. Only one play was
produced, and that by no means an extraordinary
one. But it was so well acted that the very moderate
interest of plot and dialogue counted for much more
than even the most hopeful had anticipated, and it
held its own on the Lyceum stage far into the summer,
weeks after the other stock theatres had closed their
doors. As has been intimated, the secret of this
success is not by any means to be imputed to the
authors, Mr. De Mille and Mr. Belasco. Their
work, after it had been rather remorselessly adapted
in the early weeks of the season, was effective enough ;
but it was by no means extraordinary. We have all
heard the same story told in varying terms before.
The fact about which everything revolves in "The
Wife" is the marriage of *Helen Truman* to *John
Rutherford* at a time when she had been unjustly
prejudiced against *Robert Grey*, the man she really
loved. The situation, though rather obvious, is natural
enough. In the majority of such cases, no doubt,
things go on well enough afterwards ; a previous affair

of the heart gives no positive assurance that marriage with another will be unhappy. It is, perhaps, within the limits of exactness to say that the most comfortable matches are not the issue of passion. However this may be, we all know that on the stage no such easy *dénouement* is possible. Where would be our story if there were not some evil-minded person anxious to make the most of the old wound as an irreparable and fatal pang of heart? There are, in fact, two such evil minded persons in "The Wife." One of these is a journalist without a conscience (modelled, no doubt, on the popular conviction as to the profession), and the other is a beautiful Southern girl in whom the *spretæ injuria formæ* works like a charm. She cannot have *Robert Grey* herself, and, of course, *Mrs. Rutherford* now has no use for him ; but this sensible reflection does not diminish her jealousy, and she keeps with evident enjoyment to the task of poisoning the happiness of the woman whom she still regards as her rival. The enmity of *Matthew Culver*, the journalist, springs from political quite as much as personal grounds, *Mr. Rutherford* being a member of the United States Senate, and inimical to certain schemes of his ; or, rather, it would be more accurate to say that it springs from a certain inborn malevolence of character, which is again (we must suppose) fully in keeping with his profession. A very significant quarrel between *Culver* and *Grey* at a ball in Washington is followed by a scene between these two and *Senator Rutherford* in the library of the last-named. Here the husband learns the truth as to *Grey's* love affair with his wife, and here he shows an essential manliness and generosity of disposition in a manner which it is not necessary to disclose. A touching scene with the wife succeeds the departure of the men. This third act is by far the best in the play. It is vivid and powerful, but not in the least overwrought. After this the interest in the story slowly dies out through a fourth act of slow reconciliation between husband and wife. The rather sombre narrative is enlivened throughout by humorous passages, in which *Kitty Ives*, *Jack Dexter* and *Major Homer Q. Putnam* are largely concerned.

"The Wife" was acted with a degree of skill and intelligence which deserves very high praise. Undoubtedly the highest point is reached in the interview between the three men in the library, played by Mr. Herbert Kelcey, Mr. Nelson Wheatcroft and Mr. Henry Miller. The work of each one of these excelled in force as well as finish, and was equally sincere and artistic. Mesdames Georgia Cayvan and Grace Henderson were less admirable, especially the latter, who has many disagreeable mannerisms and affectations. Miss Louise Dillon showed an exquisite and spontaneous quality of humour as *Kitty Ives*, and Mr. Lemoyne's *Major Putnam* was also well done. The acting of the other members of the company was highly commendable, and the stage-settings were very beautiful.

EDITOR.

G

DALY'S THEATRE.

[SEASON 1887-88.]

MR. AUGUSTIN DALY is frequently spoken of in our newspapers as the "foremost American manager," a title which used to be accorded to Mr. Lester Wallack, and which might justly be claimed by Mr. A. M. Palmer. The latter's brilliant record as a producer of plays, throughout an almost unbroken period of fifteen years or longer, has seldom been surpassed in this country. And something of the same distinction belongs also to Mr. Daniel Frohman, who, during his conduct of the Madison Square Theatre and the Lyceum Theatre, has shown great courage and independence in the choice of plays, has gone far to encourage American dramatists, and has demonstrated his ability as a critic of acting by his expertness in forming well-balanced companies at short notice. Mr. Frohman's present Lyceum company, though not yet a year old, is sound and charming in its elements; and this company has been admired in the most successful play of the recent season, and the brightest American play of that season, "The Wife."

Nevertheless, Mr. Daly was a "foremost" American manager before either Mr. Palmer or Mr. Frohman made himself prominent; by right of precedence, therefore, if not by right of taste superior to that of Mr. Palmer and of Mr. Frohman, he stands at the head of American managers. When Mr. Daly, after disaster overtook him in New York several years ago, departed for Europe, it was supposed that his usefulness had been drained dry. When, on returning from Europe, he produced a version of "L'Assommoir" at the Olympic Theatre, and, later, opened the house which is now known as Daly's Theatre, his prospects did not appear to be especially glowing. Yet " L'Assommoir," although it failed badly enough, introduced a clever actress to our stage, Miss Ada Rehan; and the new theatre, although for a long time it was merely a home for unsuccessful experiments, is to-day the most famous of American playhouses. It is seldom that a man enjoys in this life two distinct and equally favoured careers, the two being separated by an interregnum of failure; but Mr. Daly, as manager of the first Fifth Avenue Theatre, and at present as manager of Daly's Theatre, may be said to have carved out two careers, both successful.

Little by little Mr. Daly has built up a definite policy of management. There is no longer discord of purpose in his theatre. He does not produce a melodrama one month and a farce the next month. His productions range invariably between farce and comedy, and no one knows better than he how to present those forms of the drama with novel and delightful effect. His " new " plays are usually adaptations of German pieces, made by himself; and his adaptations reveal singular skill. They are, in fact, bright American ideas, characters, incidents, constructed, as it were, in German moulds. Occasionally Mr. Daly brings forward some fresh English piece which strikes his fancy, although his English plays are, as a rule, less happy and popular than his own. Mr. Pinero's "Dandy Dick," for example, was far less popular, and certainly far less amusing, than Mr. Daly's "Railroad of Love." Another feature of a season at Daly's Theatre is a revival of some rare old comedy, perhaps a Shaksperian comedy. Thus he revived "The Taming of the Shrew," and, more recently, "A Midsummer Night's Dream." To American dramatists Mr. Daly offers little encouragement. Mr. Bronson Howard and Mr. Edgar Fawcett are the only Americans whom he has treated with much friendliness. But it may be added that Mr. Daly hardly needs the services of our native writers for the stage.

The season of 1887-88 at Daly's Theatre began last October and ended early in April. Only three plays were produced during that season,—"Dandy Dick," "The Railroad of Love," and "A Midsummer Night's Dream." When "The Railroad of Love" was removed from the stage it was at the height of its popularity. As to the revival of "A Midsummer Night's Dream," nothing that Mr. Daly has yet done excited more interest and comment. The run of this revival was broken forcibly, for Mr. Daly had contracted to make a brief visit to Boston and to sail immediately afterwards for England. His season in London promises to be even more brilliant, if

possible, than his season in New York, even if "A
Midsummer Night's Dream" shall be replaced there
by "The Taming of the Shrew." On the whole,
however, Mr. Daly's smart and entertaining actors
appear to better advantage in "The Taming of the
Shrew." They have a keener appreciation of humour
than of poetry.

"Dandy Dick" had its first performance on the
evening of October 5th. In this piece, by one of the
br'ghtest of young English dramatists, Mr. A. W.
Pinero the principal character, that of the *Dean*, was
personated by Mr. Charles Fisher. Mr. James Lewis
appeared as *Blore*, a servant of the *Dean* ; Mr. George
Clarke as *Sir Tristram Mardon ;* Mr. John Drew
as *Major Tarver ;* Mr. Otis Skinner as *Lieut. Darby ;*
and Miss Ada Rehan as *Georgiana Tidman.* The
cast also included Mr. William Gilbert, Mr. Frederick
Bond and Miss Virginia Dreher. "Dandy Dick"
was performed only thirty-two times, and was not
worthy of the theatre in which it was performed. It
was one of those "horsey," intensely British, plays
which are seldom enjoyed by American audiences,
although they may relish such a "horsey" woman
as *Lady Gay Spanker.* The main motive of the
piece was disagreeable to the point of bad taste.
This consisted simply in making a simple-hearted
old *Dean* ridiculous. There are people who can turn
rel'gion into a joke, and this is much like turning a
disciple of Christ into a football for buffoons. Mr.
Fisher gave dignity and a kind of pathos to the
Dean, and the sincerity of his acting offered a painful
foil to the rough fun of Mr. Pinero's play. It is

somewhat surprising, indeed that Mr. Daly should have accepted such a play for his theatre, his caution in presenting only what is at the same time amusing and unobjectionable being well known. "Dandy Dick" was aggressively objectionable. Even Miss Rehan, who is seldom wrong in any good part, was not over-interesting as *Georgiana Tidman.* Her sprightly Americanism was all at odds with this character.

A failure at Daly's Theatre is an exceptional occurrence. But Mr. Daly is the last man who would strive to bolster up a failure. He recognized the fact promptly that Mr. Pinero's piece was not liked here, and he withdrew it as soon as he could. On the first day of November he produced "The Railroad of Love," which was his own adaptation of a German farce entitled "Goldfische." The cast included Miss Rehan as *Valentine Osprey,* Mrs. Gilbert as *Mrs. Laburnum,* Miss Phœbe Russell as *Viva Van Ryker,* Mr. Lewis as *Phenix Scuttleby,* Mr. Drew as *Lieut. Everett,* Mr. Clarke as *Adam Grinnedge,* Mr. Leclercq as *Judge Van Ryker,* Mr. Skinner as *Benny Dameresq* and Mr. Fisher as *Gen. Everett.*

It would be waste of ink and space to give in detail the story of such a play as "The Railroad of Love." The piece is pure farce, with a bit of spectacle here and there, and with touches of genuine comedy. It is, however, transparent almost to frivolity, and certain of its incidents are not lacking in silliness. Aside from these incidents—some of which have been used repeatedly in farce—the play is clever and amusing enough. Mr. Daly writes witty dialogue, and his best points are always excellent points. For example, he has not often written or manipulated a scene with more deftness than he has that scene in "The Railroad of Love," where *Valentine Osprey* and *Lieut. Everett*, with an open door between them, make love somewhat after the fashion of *Beatrice* and *Benedick*. This scene is of the liveliest originality, and it is the very heart of the play. The situation is not essentially new, Mr. Daly himself having treated it in one way or another several times. Mr. Daly understands his actors perfectly, and he knows that Mr. Drew and Miss Rehan are never so interesting as when they are jesting at each other's honest sentiment. Judging from their success at this blithe and harmless game, they could not fail to be particularly effective in "Much Ado about Nothing." It is learned with satisfaction, by the way, that Mr. Daly is not averse to reviving that most buoyant of great comedies.

There were one hundred and eight performances of "The Railroad of Love" at Daly's Theatre, and these might easily have been three hundred. None of Mr. Daly's adaptations—not even "Nancy and Co.," nor "7-20-8"—were more popular or more perfectly acted. Mr. Daly withdrew the piece because he was anxious to present his version of "A Midsummer Night's Dream." This revival had been looked forward to with extreme eagerness, chiefly for the reason that Mr. James Lewis was to appear as *Bottom*. Several famous *Bottoms* had been seen on the stage of New York, noticeably those of Burton, Blake, and Fox. It may be recalled that Mr. Daly revived the "Dream" at the Grand Opera House when he had charge of that theatre ; the late George L. Fox was the *Bottom* in that revival, and many old play-goers speak of his performance as one of peculiar resource and humour. The production of the play at Daly's Theatre proved to be more of a spectacle than a performance. In another place (the *Cosmopolitan Magazine,* for April) I have given a rather complete description of this spectacle ; I will confine myself at present, chiefly, to a few critical notes on the performance.

Since the cast of the play, as given at Daly's Theatre, possesses a certain historical value, I will copy it from Mr. Daly's programme :—

Theseus, Duke of Athens . . .	Mr. Joseph Holland
Egeus, father to Hermia . . .	Mr. Charles Fisher
Lysander, in love with Hermia . .	Mr. Otis Skinner
Demetrius, beloved of Helena . .	Mr. John Drew
Philostrate, master of the sports to Theseus	Mr. Eugene Ormond
Quince, the carpenter, also representing the Prologue	Mr. Charles Leclercq
Snug, the joiner, who represents also Lion	Mr. Frederick Bond
Bottom, the weaver, who likewise represents Pyramus	Mr. James Lewis
Flute, the bellows-mender, who also represents Thisbe	Mr William Gilbert
Snout, the tinker, representing Wall in the interlude	Mr. John Wood
Starveling, the tailor; also representing in the interlude, Moonshine . .	Mr. Edward Wilks
Hippolita, Queen of the Amazons, betrothed to Theseus . . .	Miss Lalla Lee
Helena	Miss Ada Rehan
Hermia	Miss Virginia Dreher
Oberon, King of the fairies . .	Miss Alice Hood
Titania, Queen of the fairies .	Miss Effie Shannon

A Fairy attending on Titania . Miss Lizzie St. Quentin
Puck, a fairy attending on Oberon . Bijou Fernandez
Other fairies, attendant upon Oberon and Titania, by Misses
Sears, Conron, Cooke, Vislaire, Ferrell, Gaunt, Wharton,
Heim, Bowne, and Page.
Attendants upon Hippolita, by Misses Lee, Berner, Ratcliffe,
Callard, Collerd, Livingston, &c. Of the Court of Theseus :
Messrs. Revell, Finney, Reglid, Keller, Murphy, Ireton, &c.

Mr. Daly made a special arrangement of "Midsummer Night's Dream" for his stage, and it must be
admitted that his arrangement was, in the main, faithful
to Shakspeare ; the original text was preserved by
him, and the cuttings and alterations were only those
which were absolutely required. His version was,
indeed, remarkably smooth and lucid. There were
five acts and seven scenes, the closing scene of the
fourth act being a panoramic illusion of the passage
of *Duke Theseus's* barge to Athens. The first scene
showed the Palace of Theseus ; the second, Quince's
workshop ; the third, a wood near Athens ; the fourth,
a moonlight view of the wood ; the fifth, Titania's
bower ; the sixth, a sunrise view of the wood ; the
seventh, an outer court of the Palace of Theseus, where
the lamentable comedy of "Pyramus and Thisbe"
was perform d. This bare statement offers no suggestion of the almost fairy-like transformations which
marked some of these scenes—the dissolving of darkness into light and of light into darkness, the sudden
glow of fireflies in opaque night, the rising and waning
of the moon, the subtle approach of dawn through
tangled forests, the splendour of luminous panorama.
The spectacle was one of unusual beauty, even if the

painting was not invariably accurate and pleasing: it suggested charmingly the mystic glamour of no-man's-land.

The acting was conscientious and, to say the least of it, humorous. If it was not all that might have been expected, it was on the right line of discriminating taste and intelligence. It was, in short, so far as it could be, a presentment of Mr. Daly's ideas. But it was not adequate acting, and, therefore, it was an imperfect presentment of those ideas. I do not agree with the many critics who assert that "A Midsummer Night's Dream" cannot be acted, that it is too illusive for the stage; although illusive, of the subtlest fibre, it was written for the stage, and it is full of theatrical devices. We may not hope to find a real fairy in the play-house, any more than we look for real suffering or real death there; but it is possible to suggest the poetic quality of a fairy, as it is possible to reproduce on the stage an essentially poetic character. The actors who are so happy in such agreeable fooling as "The Railroad of Love," however, must inevitably move in a strange atmosphere when they turn up in "A Midsummer Night's Dream." Mr. Daly's actors do nothing badly; they do some things infinitely better than they do others. The performances of Mr. Drew and Miss Rehan in "The Taming of the Shrew," were fresh, truthful, and spirited; but neither Mr. Drew nor Miss Rehan would be remembered long for what they accomplished in the "Dream." The blank verse of this play was mangled out of all its music. Miss Alice Hood, who, as *Oberon*, has lines of surpassing sweetness to utter, had no apparent appreciation of their beauty. Mr. Joseph Holland, as *Theseus*, and Miss Lalla Lee, as *Hippolyta*, were serious and stately ; but neither has yet learned the art of melodious speech —and yet what golden words were theirs ! Miss Shannon's fairy queen was pretty and colourless, and nothing could have been more grotesquely absurd than Miss Fernandez's *Puck*. It may be said for all the players whom I have mentioned that they strove with honest zeal to get the most out of their parts, and that, taking them altogether, they were inoffensive; that, of course, is a kind of negative praise which has slight value.

The " hard-handed men of Athens " were personated with quaint humour by Mr. Leclercq, Mr. Bond, Mr. Gilbert, Mr. Wood, Mr. Wilks, and Mr. Lewis. The *Quince* of Mr. Leclercq was capitally done, and the comic scenes of the play were decidedly effective. Yet it is doubtful whether Mr. Lewis's *Bottom* will go on record as a truthful performance. Granting that *Bottom* may have been a wizened, cackling, lean little fellow, there was a lack of dominant impulse in this characterization. *Quince* seemed, if anything, to be considerably more important than the unctuous and exuberant " bully." If it is right to associate with a conception of *Bottom* silliness, pomposity, self-satisfaction in the highest degree, then Mr. Lewis was not *Bottom* at all.

GEORGE EDGAR MONTGOMERY.

THE BOSTON THEATRE SHOW-PIECES.

BUILT at a time when the drama at long reach—if
I may be pardoned such an irreverent phrase about
the "legitimate" drama—was still in vogue; when
the old-fashioned comedies were still played in five
acts, and something less than forty scenes; when
the import and export of a table and two chairs was
sufficient to furnish and unfurnish a parlour, an attic
or a tap-room; when the classic tragedy had not
ceased to spout and begun to speak; when vast dis-
tances were still desired to display a tyrant's stride,
a ghost's stalk, a distracted heroine's flight, or an
ecstatic lover's rush; and when the actor's delivery,
if fine, was necessarily declamation in tragedy, and
almost outcry in comedy,—the Boston Theatre was
soon found too big for the average purposes of a
play-house, especially as real lovers of the drama—
whether before or behind the footlights—had found
more personal comfort, and greater reciprocal sympathy in the smaller buildings, which the magnificent
spaciousness of this had been expected to supersede.

Very early in its history manager and public recognized, however, that it possessed unique advantages for other entertainments. The roomy audi-
torium could receive a grand orchestra without loss of

space ; the remarkable depth from the footlights to
the curtain line gave an unprecedented perspective
to any picture set upon the stage, while the vast-
ness of that stage and the spaces subordinate
to it, gave new possibilities to spectacle and
pageant. These special qualities were not ignored,
and from time to time the dramatic performances
gave place to the opera, to the pantomime and ballet
of the Ravels, and also during a part of one season
to a splendid circus show. And the drama itself did
not disdain to profit by these conditions of construction, as was testified by the beautiful and costly productions by Mr. Barry of " The Tempest " and the
" Midsummer Night's Dream," as well as by that
gorgeous and effective old melodrama, " The Cata-
ract of the Ganges."

In later years, the stage of the Boston Theatre has
been occupied by all sorts of dramatic and musical
exhibitions—opera, Italian, German and "National ;"
tragedy, comedy, and burlesque ; lectures, concerts,
specialty shows and negro minstrelsy. These, however, have generally represented peripatetic attractions, of which each shone for a few nights or weeks,
and then vanished before a pushing successor. When
the theatre has had something which might be said
to belong there, and was directly provided by its own
managers, this something has generally been of the
spectacular nature—either a melodrama, like " Jessie
Brown " or " Michael Strogoff," or an out-and-out
show-piece, like " Jalma."

This season three such pieces have been produced
—two being revivals, viz. " The Exiles," and " The

World," and the other being a London play, "A
Run of Luck,"—the American rights having been
bought by Mr. Tompkins, who gave the first presentation of the piece in this country at the opening of
his season, on September 12th, and then kept the
piece upon the boards for three consecutive months,
when it was transferred to Niblo's in New York. Of
the former pieces nothing need be said except that
they reproduced favourite and well-known effects,
and that popular actors made up the casts, in several
instances repeating impersonations which had been
found acceptable in previous seasons.

The last named, however, brought straight from a
long and prosperous season in London, had some
features which merit chronicle. The authorship was
due to the collaboration of Mr. Henry Pettitt, a
successful playwright of the time, and Mr. Augustus
Harris, the energetic and skilful manager of Drury
Lane.

The latter had undoubtedly concerned himself chiefly
with such points as would make effect in stage setting,
action and grouping, and his skill and knowledge
were everywhere to be found and appreciated,
especially in the large and liberal mounting and
vigorous motion shown in the American reproduction
and in the ingeniously contrived revolving scenes,
whereby an edifice can be turned inside out as one
peels a banana, or transformed into a landscape as a
magician makes black white. Indeed, I should be
inclined to give to Mr. Harris higher praise than to
his co labourer, for Mr. Pettitt ought to have found
more probability, more consistency and more

humanity for his share of the joint labour ; and this
he could have done without sacrificing one iota of
the fervid domestic emotion, the filial eloquence, the
bubbling love, the ineffectual threats, the grandiloquent
defiance, the flaunting villainy and the ever-snubbed
but ultimately exalted virtue, which excite and thrill
the galleries always and occasionally arouse the
orchestra.

As the title suggests, "A Run of Luck" is a
sporting piece, and the show-scenes all derive their
motive from the field or the turf.   But the title also
suggests a series of fortunate events, which the course
of the play quite fails to produce.   In point of fact,
the general effect of the story can hardly be considered
cheerful, because almost everybody is at sixes and
sevens with fate nearly all the time, and only the
malignant, cold-blooded villain seems to meet with
any success, unless one excepts the occasional semi-
successful skirmishes of the decidedly *déclassée* young
woman he has previously deceived, who seems bent
on getting even with him, and eventually contributes
materially to his downfall.

Regarded critically, this drama merely brings into
regular relationship a set of conventional characters
whose effect upon each other can be calculated to a
nicety from the play-bill, and the result of whose
actions can be foretold from the first scene.   In brief,
one *Arthur Trevor*, the usual sporting captain of the
British novel, seems set on ruining everybody else in
the play.   He proposes to get hold of *Squire Selby's*
estate by debauching his son and getting unlimited
post obits from him, to capture the *Squire's* niece

Mabel (engaged, or about to be, to this son *George*) and marry her for her money, and then to upset a whole *Copsley* family, by getting the old gentleman into debt, obtaining possession of his favourite and promising racer, Daisy, and by making—just why, is not apparent—havoc of his daughter *Daisy's* character, and so separating her from an implacably honest young fellow known as *Copsley*, but really an elder son of *Selby* by a former wife. These multitudinous schemes of infamy are aided and abetted by the usual cockney "capper" and minor blackleg, *Charley Sandown*. Of course the girls all stick to their lovers ; young *Copsley-Selby* makes a tremendous fight for his mother's rehabilitation—her illegal marriage being proved all right—and wins ; the bad young woman helps to save the good young *Daisy*, whose flight is secured by the aid of *George Selby*, who is as very a weathercock as ever spun round among blasts of stage sin and virtue ; the race-horse, in full flesh, blood and blanket, figures a good deal as a cause of contention, but ends by winning a race and a pot of money, at which everybody but the villains and the luckless non-appearing people who laid the disastrous long odds against the filly, are delighted, and all ends with the chief characters paired of in tender embracements.

The language fluctuates from good, plain, sensible talk, to the regulation bombast, stilted and unnatural, of the sentimental melodrama of cheap theatres. The gist of the story is shown in scenes which hold together with pretty logical sequence, but in minor matters there is little cohesion or likelihood, although they all bustle along so animatedly that the spectator does not notice their lack of reason until he has got fairly out of the theatre. What fun or humour there is in the text is laboured and dull, being lugged in apparently from a sense of duty and not from any spontaneous prompting.

The popular estimate of the drama was favourable, but decidedly qualified by the unaccountable lack of discretion on the part of the American management in retaining two scenes cast unmistakably into a brothel, whither the heroine of the piece had been enticed, and where a deliberate and undisguised attempt to drug and ruin her is shown. These disgusting and shameless scenes, censured but tolerated in London and weakly passed over by most of the Boston critics, kept a great many people from the theatre; they were eventually cancelled, but too late for the play to have the success it might have obtained if it had not begun by presenting the most unnecessarily offensive situations I have seen, so far as I remember, on any Boston stage.

The separate personages have little in them to tempt actors to assume them, in spite of the admitted effectiveness of their combination; indeed it is on record that Mr. Charles Warner refused the hero's part in the London production. Miss Minnie Radcliffe and Miss Lillian Lee were sympathetic as the girls, *Daisy* and *Mabel;* Miss Grace Thorne showed decided force as *Lucy Byfield, Trevor's* discarded, revengeful sweetheart; Miss Rosa France was a pretty *Phœbe;* and Mrs. W. G. Jones made a good deal of the *Squire's* sister, *Aunt Mary.* Among the men of the cast there

II

can be noted for correctness and care, Mr. Forrest Robinson and Mr. Ross as the young *Copsley* and *Selby*, Mr. Losee as *Trevor*, Mr. F. E. Lamb as the hostler *Jim*, an especially good bit of work, Mr. Crompton as the elder *Copsley*, and Mr. Maguinnis as *Sandown*, in which he did miracles of labour in working out all the fun which the authors allowed to creep into the piece. Some minor changes were made in the cast during the run, but no acting of consequence was thereby brought out.

The exciting scenes of the play were those in which the horses and dogs appeared. The meet at the end of the third act introduced the full force of both, and the curtain fell on a busy pack of eager hounds held well in discipline by a professional huntsman and a picturesque group of equestrians. As the play proceeded, the special horse, *Daisy*, had several times occasion to be shown, and at the finale an exceedingly well managed effect was had by simulating the finish of the eventful race; the several horses were ridden at a hand gallop across the back scene, the great breadth of the stage allowing a brisk pace to be gotten up conveniently.

Of course the interior situations lost all domesticity and homelikeness in the bald, gaunt setting of the wilderness of a stage upon which two or three people in plain, familiar talk are almost as helpless as they look. But the principal out-door scenes were well peopled, and the grouping and pantomime intentions were good and to the point. There was no chance for brilliant scenery, but the eye was gratified by just perspective, harmonious colour and appropriate landscape in the larger drops, while the smaller set pieces were correct in character and execution. A great deal of attention was paid to minor details, but some of these were not modelled after English originals, and therefore incongruities were unnecessarily forced upon the observation and criticism of whoever happened to know England. These defects were all the more to be regretted, because they not only diminished the accuracy but also the picturesqueness of the piece.

HOWARD MALCOM TICKNOR.

THE BOSTON MUSEUM.

UNDOUBTEDLY the most successful play of the forty-seventh regular season at the Museum was the " Bells of Haslemere," which was produced, for the first time in this country, on Monday evening, February 6th, 1888. It need hardly be pointed out, however, that as a work of art "The Bells of Haslemere" is altogether inferior to other plays presented at this house, such as "Sophia,' and "The Red Lamp." The record for the entire season is as follows :— "The Dominie's Daughter," Monday, August 29th, 1887; "The Red Lamp," Monday, September 19th; "Diplomacy," Monday, October 3rd; "The Guv'nor," Monday, October 10th; "Simpson & Co." and "Oliver Twist," Saturday, October 15th; "Sophia," Monday, October 17th; "The Barrister," Monday, November 28th; "The Soggarth," Monday, December 19th; "Dandy Dick," Monday, January 16th, 1888; "The Magistrate," Monday, January 30th; "A Conjugal Lesson," and "Still Waters Run Deep," Thursday, February 2nd; and "The Bells of Haslemere," Monday, February 6th, which lasted out the season until the engagement of Madame Janauschek on April 16th and of Mr. Mansfield on May 7th.

The Dominie's Daughter," selected for the

initial production of the season, is a play of colonial times, written by Mr. David D. Lloyd, the scene being laid in New York city at the time of the occupation by Sir Henry Clinton. It appears that *Molly Van Derveer*, whose father is a loyal American minister, and whose brother is in the Continental army, is beloved by *Captain Dyke* and *Major Barton*, both of the British army. She loves the former, but the latter schemes to secure her hand, places *Captain Dyke* in a false position towards the lady by compelling him, as a subordinate officer, to arrest Miss Van Derveer and her father for treason, and her brother, who has come into the city on an errand of war, as a spy. The brother escapes, and, to secure the release of her father from prison, *Molly* promises to become the wife of *Major Barton*. She holds to her promise to the last, but *Barton*, at the very church door, sees how things stand and abdicates in favour of his rival. This is distinctly the weak point of the play, and the author has recognized this by providing an alternative ending, which was tried at the Museum on Wednesday evening, September 7th, and was generally accepted as an improvement upon the original version. For if *Major Barton* is to do one good act at the last, we should be clearly made to perceive at the outset that spark of virtue in him which keeps generous impulses warm, even among the dishonourable expedients to which passion and opportunity drive him. But the cool, calculating villain for which we are supposed to accept him, could hardly abandon all his evil designs at once for a mere sentiment. The second method employed, which is

simply to make his opponent the agent in his downfall, is simpler, saner and infinitely more coherent
dramatically.   As to the merits and defects of " The
Dominic's Daughter," regarded as a whole, little need
be said.   The play is neither very good nor very
bad.   There are many excellent qualities in it, but
on the whole its merits are obscured by crude construction.   It is exceedingly talky, and the movement
drags throughout.   The character moves up and
down in see-saw fashion, and there is scarcely a moment during the progress of the play when it is not
possible to predict exactly what the next incident
will be and what characters will next appear.   Much
of the dialogue is very bright, and some of it sparkles
with wit; it is rarely heavy, though some of the
longer speeches intended to be patriotic are turgid
and almost bombastic.   Still, the great faults of the
play are its uneven and sluggish movement and in
several instances its inartistic and clumsily managed
situations.   The second act is conspicuous in this
respect.   It is certainly incongruous, and indeed not
even dramatically necessary, for two British officers
to waylay a young lady on the green in front of the
church on a summer afternoon, in order to propose
to her.   Neither do we think that a Continental spy
would openly parade and discuss his plans in the
same place and at the same time, with the full knowledge that the British troops are on the watch for
him.

The piece is well presented by the Museum company.   In our opinion, Miss Evesson is at once the
central and the most charming figure in the perfor-

mance, and her impersonation of the young woman who gives the play its name is thoroughly admirable in its mixture of sweetness, grace, delicacy and womanly courage. In the trying finale of the third act Miss Evesson displays very considerable dramatic strength. Mrs. Vincent's interpretation of *Mrs. Beekman* will long be remembered by those who had the pleasure to see it as the last character ever taken by her, since it was at the very beginning of the season that this admirable actress, so long a favourite in Boston, was taken suddenly ill and died. Her place in the play was filled by Madame Ponisi, from Wallack's Theatre. None of the other characters in "The Dominie's Daughter" require anything but the briefest comment. Mr. Barron as *Captain Dyke* gives one of those well-studied bits of acting for which he is distinguished, albeit the character itself is somewhat colourless and weak. The *Major Barton* of Mr. Frazer Coulter, the *Lieutenant Robert Van Derveer* of Mr. E. L. Davenport, and the *Rev. John Van Derveer* of Mr. Hudson are severally sufficiently well done to answer the demands of the parts. Mr. Wilson has a congenial *rôle* in *Hiram Brown*, the quaint humour of which he brings out very strongly.

The first representation in this country of a play which has been conspicuously successful across the water is naturally second in interest to the production of an entirely new work. The dramatic taste—or too often want of taste—of playgoers on both sides of the Atlantic has been cultivated to an almost equal extent, and "Hoodman Blind" can be counted upon to please New York audiences as greatly as "Shadows

of a Great City" to interest audiences in London.
This community of feeling has its obvious advantages
which need not now be discussed. We would not
wish to be understood as comparing "The Red
Lamp" with either of the pieces named; but by the
principle to which we have referred, it ought to have
been one of the successes of the Museum season.
The critics, however, for the most part fell upon it
with so much more vigour than discretion, that it was
withdrawn after only two weeks of life. The play
had better luck in London, where it was first produced in April, 1887, at the Comedy Theatre, of
which Mr. Beerbohm-Tree was then the temporary
manager. It kept the stage of that cosy little house
until late in July, and was afterwards revived for a
time at the Haymarket after Mr. Tree took the
management of that house. The substantial popularity which "The Red Lamp" has enjoyed across
the water is, on the whole, deserved. It is not a
great play, but it is a clever one; and the stage has
seen so much dramatic bungling of late that cleverness alone is something for which we should be
profoundly grateful. The scene of the place is St.
Petersburg, and its atmosphere, we need hardly add,
is Nihilism. The underground plottings of the con-
spirers against the Tsar are rather vividly portrayed,
particularly in one intensely absorbing act—while
here and there are introduced very picturesque
touches illustrating the terrorism upon which the
Russian autocracy is based. The motive of "The
Red Lamp" is the enforced disloyalty of the *Princess Claudia Morakoff*, who, though a relentless

enemy of Nihilism, is forced to become its accessory by finding her dearly-loved brother concerned in one of its secret conspiracies. The machinations of a shrewd old police agent on the one hand, and a treacherous conspirator on the other, lead her into desperate straits, from which she is rescued only by the native good sense of an American journalist, who is her daughter's lover. All this, as the reader will observe, is well-worn dramatic material; but it is so cleverly used that the spectator is at once impressed with the freshness, as well as the fertility, of the author's invention. And, indeed, it would be doing Mr. Outram Tristram an injustice to assert that the bare outline of his work which we have given is in any sense an accurate measure of its value, which lies not so much in the central idea of the play as in the admirable ingenuity with which the subsidiary incidents are developed. The entire second act, for instance, shows the author to be possessed of the faculty of invention and expedient in no small degree, while the climax of the third act, where the American foils the detective with a dose of his own medicine— his favourite excuse, "a whim, merely a whim"—is particularly ingenious and effective. At the same time, "The Red Lamp" has no striking artistic interest, nor does it embody any distinct æsthetic impulse. Its art is the art of Du Boisgobey and Gaboriau ; but in an age oppressed by Pettitt and Sims this is not a fault for which we can find no excuse. In the comedy of intrigue—to which, with a certain added intensity of human passion, "The Red Lamp" belongs—the cardinal sin against art is

dulness; and of this Mr. Tristram is certainly not
guilty. With the exception of a certain heaviness
which pervades the beginning of the play, he has
displayed great cleverness throughout.

There is a general lack of spirit in the acting of
the Museum company in this play. This criticism
applies particularly to Mr. Barron, whose impersonation of *Demetrius*, the crafty old detective, needs
especially the saving grace of elasticity. Mr. Barron's
conception of the part is excellent in every other
respect than this. The shuffling, stealthy gait, the
dry, watchful manner, the face impassive save for the
watchful eyes, convey to the intelligence of the
spectator with admirable distinctness the inward
character of the man. So far, too, as Mr. Barron's
speech and bearing are deliberate, he is equally in
keeping with the *Demetrius* of the author; but the
effect of monotony which he produces is not happy.
In the hands of Mr. Beerbohm-Tree the old fox has
about double the dramatic value which Mr. Barron
gives him. To Miss Clarke, who takes the trying
part of the *Princess Claudia Morakoff*, well-nigh
unstinted praise should be given. She makes the
woman who is so cruelly tortured between the spirit
of patriotism and the impulse of affection both consistent and vivid in the imagination of the spectator,
which is a great deal more than Lady Monckton,
who originally essayed the part, was ever able to do.
In fact, Miss Clarke does much more than merely
interpret the thought of the dramatist; she makes a
character in some respects conventional thoroughly
human with the warmth and fulness of nature itself.

Few of those who have seen her impersonation, we venture to say, can ever forget her superb attitude of defiance before the detective when he accuses her before her husband, or the instant alteration of her face from defiance to triumph when he is compelled to place the red lamp, the signal of safety to the Nihilists, in the accustomed window. There is the exercise of the prerogative of royal blood in every gesture. The tenderness of the *Princess* for her daughter and her brother is also admirably exhibited ; and taken all in all, the impersonation demands that superlative commendation which the critic very seldom has occasion to apply. The other members of the company—with the exception of Miss Evesson, who is sweetness and grace itself in the comparatively colourless *rôle* of the daughter—do not rise to distinction. Mr. Seymour makes of the journalist an impossible compound of audacity and good-nature, and Mr. Coulter is traditionally villainous as the Russian journalist. Mr. E. L. Davenport plays the part of the *Prince* with taste and feeling, and Mr. Hudson is rather explosive and uncouth as the military husband of the *Princess*. The stage settings, though not elaborate, are very handsome.

Between the withdrawal of "The Red Lamp" and the production of "Sophia," several plays which are too familiar to need comment, were presented. In "Diplomacy" the practically new impersonations were those of Mr. E. L. Davenport and Miss Isabelle Evesson ; the one as *Julian Beauclerc*, the other as *Dora*. There was a large compensation for Mr. Davenport's inexperience in the remarkable artistic insight and dramatic vigour which he displayed ; and Miss Evesson deserves hearty praise for an exquisite combination of sweetness and genuine feeling. Having said this much, we pass on to a brief consideration of "Sophia." This play, as every one knows, is a dramatization of Fielding's novel, "Tom Jones." We should like to write Fielding's familiar novel ; but we fear that the self-constituted censorship of morals at the Boston Public Library (and other similar institutions, no doubt) has made the epithet impossible. It is much safer to say of one of the most brilliant of English novelists what was once said with truth of the greatest of English dramatists—that every one talks about him and no one reads him. With that self-sufficient class of modern writers to whom Thackeray is already a barbarian, Fielding is a hissing and a byword. How much of the well-nigh utter neglect into which he has fallen is due to the rigid propriety of the age, we will not attempt in this place to discuss ; but it may be remarked in passing that it is doubtful if we are so very much the superior of our ancestors in virtue, and that our rage is not so much against vice as against vice unadorned. Fielding is tabooed, but we do not find that "Ouida" is yet altogether a literary outcast. This is, however, somewhat aside from the question of the merits of Mr. Buchanan's play, which can never for a moment raise any ethical suspicions in the mind of the most prudent. Mr. Buchanan has left us a hint of the fact that *Tom Jones* is a sad dog ; but his specifications (outside of the *Lady Bellaston* incident) are so vague that they carry little positive conviction. Besides, *Tom's* conduct toward *Lady Bellaston* is made on the whole so irreproachable, and his treatment·of *Molly Segrim* (another inconvenient episode) is so blameless, that he fairly poses throughout the play in an attitude not unbecoming the virtuous hero of melodrama. It is here, perhaps, that Mr. Buchanan has erred on the side of delicacy; though leaving the literary and taking the purely dramatic point of view, it is difficult to say what other course was open to him. It was obviously impossible that he should make *Tom Jones* all that Fielding made him; idealization was absolutely necessary; but at the same time the purifying process may possibly have been carried too far. We do not mean by this that we·would have liked to see the play made coarse or vulgar; but there is always a danger to real strength and virility in the process of Bowdlerizing, and this danger Mr. Buchanan has not altogether escaped. But it would be unfair, on the other hand, not to recognize the fact that he has preserved the healthy, hearty atmosphere of the novel to a gratifying extent, and that he has left *Tom Jones* himself a good share of the essential manliness and honour with which his creator endowed him. It is upon *Sophia Weston*, however, that the interest of the play largely depends; Mr. Buchanan is entirely right in his assertion that that gracious figure "dominates his drama as it really dominates the novel." There are few more lovable characters in all English fiction than she; we must come to Thackeray's Laura Pendennis before we find one who can compare with her in maidenly faithfulness and purity. The blackness of the world around her only makes more radiant her whiteness of soul. This world of rakes of both sexes Mr. Buchanan has transferred from the novel to the play with admirable fidelity and discretion. *Squire Weston*, *Lady Bellaston*, *Molly Seagrim*, and *Blifil* step down from their eighteenth-century frames into our modern atmosphere, and give even the spectator who is unacquainted with his Fielding a taste of that master-spirit. And the far more genial figures of *Allworthy* and *Partridge* become once more vivid and instinct with life to the reader who cherishes for them an affectionate remembrance.

The performance of " Sophia " at the Museum is rather exasperatingly good and bad. It is not a pleasant task to find fault with so capable an actor as Mr. Barron ; but we are compelled to observe that for the dull moments of the piece he is largely responsible. It goes without saying that his impersonation of *Tom Jones* is sincere, strong and in its way artistic ; but it is sincerity without lightness of touch, strength without flexibility and art without eloquence. The essentially robust quality of the character is hardly suggested ; the animal good spirits, the pulsing manly passions, the rough directness and candour of the man are not brought at all vividly before the spectator. Refinement is an excellent, an essential thing in art ; but the native underlying power must not be rubbed away. Mr. Barron's *Tom Jones*, with all its obvious merits, has a thinness and meagreness that robs it of its real impressiveness and vigour. Mr. Davenport's interpretation of the difficult part of *Blifil*, on the other hand, has all the qualities of concentration and force of conception which one missed in *Tom Jones*. His artistic reserve is remarkable in so young an actor, and only once does he really lose his grasp upon the character. Miss Evesson is an ideal *Sophia* in personal appearance ; and, although in one or two critical moments she falls far short of ideal force and fervour, she nevertheless reaches a point of sympathetic feeling which atones in part for her fault. In the quieter moments of the play she is exquisitely natural, and gives renewed promise of that growth in her art which has characterized her career in Boston. Miss Clarke is admirable as the brilliant but debased *Lady Bellaston*, and her final scene is memorable in its brazen cynicism. Mr. Wilson has a congenial task in portraying the barber, *Partridge*, and his characteristically rich and genial humour never served him in better stead. Miss Dayne makes a light and deft *Honour*, and Mrs. Farren is conventionally good as *Tabitha Weston.* Of Mr. Seymour as the *Squire*, of Miss Davenport as *Mollie Seagrim* and of Mr. Nolan as *Square* it is impossible to say much in praise. Mr. Seymour, in particular, misses the racy flavour of the soil with which the country magnate is redolent. The play is prettily put upon the stage.

" The Barrister," is three long acts of farce, pure and simple, without a touch of genuine comedy. It is of precisely the same pattern as " The Magistrate," and scores of other plays, either imported outright or " conveyed " from various sources during the past few years. The necessary materials are a marital complication, a confusion of identity and a tangle of irreconcilable ideas. A number of persons of no especial distinctness of character serve as the puppets which conveniently dance when the author pulls the strings, and involve and then extricate themselves with a precision never attained by actual human beings. How all these entanglements are finally disposed of it is not our intention to relate. Unless we are very much mistaken, we have already told enough to indicate the precise artistic value of the play, of which we can only say, in conclusion, that it is *vox et præterea nihil.* It has nothing in common either with nature or with art; it is simply a clever game of dramatic checkers. The dialogue, it should in justice be added, is neat and bright, and some of the repartees have the flavour of nice wit. The acting in "The Barrister," it may be briefly said, is quite as good as the play. "The Soggarth," an Irish play, of which Mr. George Darrell is the author, merits the adjective "romantic," in so far that incident, out and away beyond character, is important in its composition. Indeed, "The Soggarth" is rich in situation, incident, effect. In the first act, Castle Glenmore, on its hill, makes a noble background for the birthday feast and the dance; the absentee landlord returns, and Saxon and Celt meet in the persons of *Lord Glenmore* and *Neil Maguire;* and soon the assembling of the tenants and the eviction (as it were) of the tyrannous agent move the spectator after a similar fashion. Of the play itself there is really very little to say. The plenitude of incident and accident has already been pointed out. For the rest, "The Soggarth" is a commonplace drama, with far too little humour to relieve its mediocre tragedy. The characters impress themselves as types rather than as individuals, and this, with a curious dispersal of interest, keeps any one person from holding long or firmly the sympathy of the spectator. The one opportunity for acting under uncommon conditions falls to Mr. Hudson, because, as the *Soggarth*, he was called upon to show the conflict in one soul between priest and man. If Mr. Hudson makes by no means the most of this opportunity—as he surely does not—it is at least to be said that he does not ruin it by exaggeration. Mr. Barron is dignified and grave as *Lord Glenmore;* Mr. Wilson's "saving grace of humour" keeps him, for the most part, from overdoing his unfamiliar part of villain ; and Mr. Davenport, in the character of *Neil Maguire*, although perhaps too demonstrative, is earnest and strong. Miss Clarke's *Lady Ruby Pontifex*—a name worthy of Lord Beaconsfield's imagination in its prime—is all that the part demanded ; Miss Evesson does some things in her best manner as *Neil Maguire's* sister ; and Miss Ryan makes an undoubted hit with her *Elsie Maginnis.*

"Dandy Dick," which followed "The Soggarth" at the Museum, was the opening piece of the season at Daly's Theatre, New York ; and there, as seen, despite its long run at the Court Theatre, London, it was unsuccessful. As a brief criticism of "Dandy Dick" is to be found in the article dealing with the productions of the year at Daly's Theatre, it will be only necessary in this place to make some reference to the acting of the Museum company. Miss Clarke deserves to be mentioned first for her marvellously fine and true impersonation of *Georgina*

I

Tidman, who is a sort of doubly-distilled *Lady Gay Spanker*, which would carry through successfully a much worse piece than "Dandy Dick." She impersonates the "horsey" widow with great adroitness and brilliancy, and is brisk, pungent and just a little "loud," without descending to mere *brusquerie* or coarseness. Mr. Barron does more satisfactory work as *Sir Tristram Mardon* than in any other part he has attempted this season except that of *Captain Vere* in "The Bells of Haslemere," and deserves commendation similar in kind, and only less in degree, to that won by Miss Clarke. A charming feature of the performance is Miss Isabelle Evesson's impersonation of *Sheba*, one of the daughters of the poor harassed old *Dean*. It was rich in unforced humour, genuine naïveté and easy spontaneity. Miss Evesson has done nothing better since her exquisite work in "Held by the Enemy" last year, and this is saying a good deal for one whose touch is always light and graceful, and who combines all the advantages of youth and beauty with the delicacy and insight of the true artist. Miss Dayne is disappointing as the other daughter, though she, too, has moments of lucidity and ease. Mr. Hudson does very well indeed in the rather unsympathetic part of the *Dean*, though he never reaches absolute distinction. Mr. Wilson is dryly humorous as *Blore*, the old butler, and Miss Ryan does her small part with some success, but Mr. Seymour and Mr. Davenport are not very amusing in their attempts to portray two brainless officers, and Mr. Nolan is quite too silly as the jealous *Constable*.

In the week between the withdrawal of "Dandy Dick" and the production of "The Bells of Hasle-mere," "The Magistrate," familiar to every theatre-goer, and "Still Waters run Deep," one of the late Tom Taylor's comedies, which is so seldom played as to have all the novelty and zest of a new piece were given. The plot of "Still Waters run Deep" is drawn from Charles de Bernard's novel, "Le Gendre;" and the play may unhesitatingly be called one of the very best specimens of the English drama of a generation or two ago. It has not quite the touch of the great age of unpoetic comedy—an age that produced "She Stoops to Conquer" and "The School for Scandal;" it is less vivid in characterization and less brilliant in dialogue, though still near to nature and to art. All subtle distinctions aside, however, plays like "Still Waters run Deep" have enough genuine dramatic merit to lift them to the rank of classics beside the slipshod and vulgar work of modern playwrights. Taylor has a fine and delicate touch reminding one not a little of such masters in the French school as Scribe, Labiche and Legouvé (though we are far from assigning to these three an equal place in their art), and the development of the story is accompanied by some very clever drawing of human nature. *Brother Potter* and *Mrs. Sternhold* deserve no mean place in one's gallery of theatrical recollections. And Mr. Hudson and Miss Clarke each do brilliant and finished work in their respec-tive impersonations of these characters. Mr. Barron is too dry and perfunctory as *Mildmay*, and Miss Evesson, though always agreeable, is unsuited to the part of *Mrs. Mildmay.* It may be interesting to remember that " Still Waters run Deep " was first brought out in Boston at the Howard Athenæum, in 1855, with Mr. Brown as *Mildmay*, J. M. Field as *Hawksley*, E. B. Williams as *Potter*, Mrs. W. H. Smith as *Mrs. Sternhold*, and Mrs. J. M. Field as *Mrs. Mildmay.* A month later the piece was given at the Museum for Mr. William Warren's benefit, with Mr. Warren as *Mildmay*, Mr. Keach as *Hawksley*, Mr. Joyce as *Potter*, Mrs. Vincent as *Mrs. Sternhold*, and Mrs. Skerrett as *Mrs. Mildmay.* In 1865 it was revived, when Mr. Shewell appeared as *John Mildmay*, Mr. E. L. Davenport as *Hawksley*, Mrs. Davenport as *Mrs. Sternhold*, and Miss Fanny Davenport as *Mrs. Mildmay.*

Really good and substantial melodrama is rather refreshing after the farce-comedy and riotous horse-play with which we are usually afflicted at the theatres in these days ; and even those whose tastes lead them to prefer Shakspeare or Sheridan or Goldsmith to Mr. Sims or Mr. Jones or Mr. Pettitt can bear with a certain equanimity the delight of the audiences at the Museum in " The Bells of Haslemere." It is a better play than its predecessor at the Adelphi Theatre in London, " The Harbour Lights," which was also the great success of last season at the Museum. Between the two plays there is little to choose, perhaps, in the way of actual fidelity to nature or of absolute relation (or, rather, lack of relation) to art ; but in a certain dramatic compactness in the development of the plot and in clearness and vividness of motive the later of the two seems to us to be in every way superior

Indeed, "The Bells of Haslemere" will compare favourably with the bulk of modern melodramas in being less obviously built around certain scenes and mechanical devices for which the stage manager rather than the playwright is responsible. It is by no means bare of scenic effect; but this feature is more an incident than an essential of the production. We may be doing Mr. Pettitt an injustice, but we have a suspicion that his collaborator, Mr. Sydney Grundy, deserves the greater share of the credit for this result. Mr. Grundy has always shown the keener eye for artistic values, as distinguished from the mere use of sliding scenes and lime lights; and in those portions of "The Bells of Haslemere" where something of a dramatic intuition and a literary faculty work together in happy combination we fancy that his hand may be readily detected. So far as the story in its essential features goes, there is little strength or originality. The framework is precisely that of every other melodrama in which writers of the Pettitt order have ever had a hand. The virtuous young squire is the central figure, and immediately revolving around him are the simple village maiden to whom his heart is given, the honest rustic who is his devoted friend through thick and thin, and the guileless victim of the Squire's bad enemy who unselfishly runs any risk to save that virtuous gentleman at the proper moment. He is naturally pursued by a brace of heartless scoundrels, one the tool and finally the assassin of the other. Along with these is a third scoundrel who has a few amiable instincts, which come to help along the destruction of vice and the glorification of virtue. In the third act, which occurs on a Southern plantation, there is a singularly noble and unselfish young girl, who is more than half in love with the outcast hero, and who manages to save his life when he is pursued even in that remote spot by the machinations of the deadliest villain of all. This portion of the play is really fresh and interesting, and the character of this girl, *Norah Desmond*, is drawn with a singularly graceful and sympathetic touch, quite worthy of the author of " In Honour Bound." The Yankee captain has also a quality of rough manliness which is not unskilfully portrayed. Several of the passages in this portion of the play have the humour which is seldom visible in English melodrama ; and we are willing to venture the surmise that the entire act is largely, if not altogether, the work of Mr. Grundy. In the fourth and last act we are once again in Mr. Pettitt's familiar province, and in the complicated melodramatic mechanism of the scene in the library, at the forge and at the mill-race we can almost imagine that ingenious gentleman pulling the strings. For the scenery in these two acts a hearty word of praise is demanded. The earlier scenes lack imagination and softness of colour, and the eye educated by Mr. Irving cannot accept the representation of the manor house and its surroundings as an artistic bit of English landscape. But the bayou, the cane brake and the swamp are in every way admirably represented.

Enough has been said of " The Bells of Haslemere," we fancy, to give the reader a pretty just idea of its general scope, as well as of its individual faults or

merits. At any rate, it is not necessary to follow the
story in detail. As we have already indicated, the
play has its substantial merits, considered as a melodrama, and there are not a few detached scenes and
passages which may fairly be praised without even
this reservation. The acting may be commended
very warmly in most instances. Mr. E. L. Davenport
takes the chief part, that of the *Squire of Haslemere.*
In certain crucial moments he falls short of that
degree of excellence which a more experienced actor
might easily have attained. More than this, his
impersonation lacks both variety and solidity, and is
alternately too intense and too impassive. But when
all these deductions—and they are serious ones—
have been made, there remains the very important
quality of temperamental artistic insight and force,
which Mr. Davenport possesses in a distinct degree,
and which gives his work a peculiar interest to the
thoughtful spectator. This quality serves him best
in those moments of quiet pathos which are less in-
herently melodramatic than the conventional passages
given over to denunciatory vehemence. The greatest
success is won by Miss Miriam O'Leary. The mixture of ardour and shrewdness in the character of
Norah Desmond was cleverly indicated by her, and in
the scene where she more than half confesses her
growing *tendresse* for the young squire the mingled
pathos and humour of the situation were exquisitely
portrayed. Here her anxiety to learn the relationship of the squire's correspondent to himself is
delightfully and beautifully manifested in the finely
discriminating manner of her utterance of the three

successive questions : " Your sister ? Your mother ?
Your wife ? "   Her raillery of her jealous lover, her
appeal to his manliness and honour to save the squire
and her defiance of the pursuers are each and all
admirable.   Mr. Frazer Coulter appears as the deep-
est-dyed villain of the whole malodorous gang, and
acts with impressiveness and fidelity (so far as the
part allows him) to nature.   Mr. Wilson is excellent
in many respects as *Reuben Armstrong*, the black-
smith, though his impersonation has little of the
flavour of the soil.   Miss Evesson, just as last year in
" The Harbour Lights," again has to portray the
feminine prig, a task strangely out of consonance
with her bright, genial and beautifully natural artistic
method.   She does this with dignity and fervour, and
makes at all times a sweet and gracious picture to
the eye ; but the part is far beneath the scope of her
ability.   Miss Maida Craigen, too, has to repeat her
experience of a year ago in giving life and coherence
to the character of the young schoolmistress who
poses as the victim of villainy.   Miss Craigen is a
refined and thoroughly conscientious actress, but she
has not so far in her brief career upon the stage
reached any very high pitch of artistic achievement.
But she deserves moderate praise for her efforts to
make something out of next to nothing in the
character of *Mary Northcote*.   Mr. Barron's impersonation of the cynical rascal, *Captain Vere*, is
thoroughly admirable in its cool insolence and
audacity ; Mr. Falkland displays sincerity and skill
in his portrayal of the conventional representation
of the better sort of villager, in this case an honest

but fiery young miller; Mr. Boyd Putnam shows a certain rough strength as the Yankee captain; and Mr. Nolan, Mr. Sidney, and Miss Dayne fill out the cast more or less agreeably.

EDITOR.

MR. HARRIGAN'S LATEST PLAY.

THE season at Mr. Harrigan's ever-popular Park
Theatre in New York was mainly devoted to a new
play, " Pete," from the hands of that actor.   It was
first produced in November, 1887, and it ran well into
the spring, and was then taken "on tour" to Boston
and other places.   But " Pete " is not a good play.
Mr. Harrigan's efforts as a writer have been principally
given to plays that reflect, often with great truth, a
certain level and corner of New York life ; and as an
actor he is chiefly known for his skilful rendering of
Irish parts.   The action of " Pete," however, passes
in the South, and every class of society—from rich
planters down to negroes and poor whites—appears in
its scenes.   The first act opens with the marriage of
Colonel Randolph Coolidge to a lady whose pretended
brother, *Victor Lemaire*, is soon discovered by the
audience—though not by his fellow *personæ*—to be not
her brother, but her lover. *Dr. Joseph Clifford*, a
friend of *Coolidge's*, arrives too late for the wedding,
but in time to tell his friend that a mock-marriage
which the *Colonel* had entered into was real, and that,
therefore, a certain *Mary Morgan* is his wife, and not
the beautiful *Marie*.   The spectator is called upon to
believe that these two Southern gentlemen keep still

about the affair, and let things go on as if it had not happened.   Old *Pete*, however, hears their talk, and does not forget.   Almost immediately news is brought that a poor white woman, a stranger, has died in *Aunt Charlotte's* cabin, after giving birth to a child ; then comes the tidings that Fort Sumter has been fired on ; and *Coolidge* and *Clifford* go soldiering, one to the North and the other in the South, while *Lemaire* remains with his guilty love.   The reader will observe that neither *Coolidge* nor *Marie* is entitled to the balance of pity, as each has deceived the other.   Out of all this intricate promise of complexities to come, which is given in the first act, is developed a story which shall not be told here.

Enough has been said, without spoiling the pleasure of those who are greedy of plots, to show the main drift of " Pete ;" and it is a poor play, not only because a conventional plot is worked out with halts and hitches, but because its types of Southern gentlefolk are such as flourish in third-rate novels.   An Irish alderman and his wife are caricatures, but caricatures in the line of truth, and the negroes are what we have always been taught to believe them.   It is these characters, the glimpses of plantation life, and above all, Mr. Braham's songs—in which he has been extraordinarily true to the spirit of negro melody—that give " Pete " its long-continued success.

The acting is better than the play, but only one or two of the performers demand special note.   Mr. Harrigan has given himself an *Uncle Tom* part, which he plays with a fairly good vernacular, and with the skill and attention to detail that distinguish most of his work. Mr. Dan Collyer gives a remarkable picture of a half-crazed negro girl, to whom an attendance upon the Voodoo mysteries has imparted a touch of weirdness; Mrs. Yeamans, as the alderman's wife, executes one of her realistic and extraordinarily clever bits in this presentment of the sort of Irish woman we all know too well; and Mr. Coffey's *Shadrack*, the wicked negro who struggles with the black bacchante on the night of the child's rescue, deserves a separate word. No one else does any noteworthy acting, but the songs and dances are given with admirable spirit and zest. One could listen more than once to "The Old Barn Floor," "Slavery's Passed Away," and "The Old Black Crow," and yet wish to hear them again. The scenery is elaborate, and often effective; and a steamboat, two oxen and a mule keep up the credit of realism.

C. T. COPELAND.

A DRAMA OF ANARCHY.

[PAUL KAUVAR.]

THE dramatic work of Mr. Steele Mackaye always bears the stamp of a strong and interesting individuality. It may be true that he sometimes borrows his plots and situations, but it cannot be disputed that when he chooses to make use of old material he treats it with so much boldness, originality and force that it often assumes the appearance of novelty. He is endowed with both dramatic and theatrical instinct, possessing not only a keen appreciation of all possibilities of stage effect, but that fine literary and artistic sense which discriminates between what is merely startling to the eye or ear and the conditions which stir the heart or exercise the understanding. In all his plays there has been an intellectual quality, together with great vigour and directness of purpose, which has elevated them to a plane far above that occupied by the ordinary comedy or melodrama of the day, and these same characteristics are manifest to an uncommon degree in " Paul Kauvar, or Anarchy," which was presented for the first time in New York in the Standard Theatre, in December last, before a large audience, which was always interested and attentive, and was aroused more than once to great enthusiasm. It may be said at once that it won a pronounced success on its merits, in spite of several grave faults.

The piece may be described briefly as a romantic melodrama of the time of the French Revolution. Its original title, "Anarchy," was a misnomer, and created false impressions. Anarchy does not now furnish the reason or motive of the play, but is made to supply some striking tableaux and incidents, and the idea that it might furnish a fascinating title also, in view of recent events in this country, was natural enough. Second thoughts, which are best sometimes, probably led to the reflection that the theme was not the most pleasing in the world ; that disquisitions concerning it would be unprofitable and justification of it impossible, and that it would be wisest to introduce it only as a sort of lurid background to the prominent figures in the plot. It is understood that the work has been modified in several respects since its earliest trial in Buffalo, but it is not necessary to affect concern for what occurred in that remote locality. What remains is melodrama of a remarkably virile, imaginative, and effective kind, which leaves all problems, philosophical or social, severely alone, except when the hero indulges in a high-flown platitude or two about the beauties of freedom or patriotism.

The story is so involved that anything like an intelligible synopsis of it would be likely to prove very tedious, but it is put together so compactly and ingeniously that no confusion is left in the mind of the spectator. The construction, indeed, is thoroughly workmanlike throughout. There are incidents enough in the five acts to fill half a dozen ordinary plays, and

if most of them have been long familiar in different
forms of fiction, they are, at least, newly-arranged.
The most obvious criticism to be passed upon the
work as a whole is that it is keyed up to too high a
tension. There is scarcely a trial or peril within the
limits of human experience to which the hero and
heroine are not subject. Never was such an aggrega-
tion of agony upon agony. Poor *Paul* has endured
almost every variety of mental torture before he is
carried off at the end of the second act to die upon
the guillotine, whereupon he proposes to offer himself
a vicarious sacrifice, after the example of *Sydney Carton ;* but all this preparatory experience is as nothing
to the whirlwind of tempestuous emotions by which
he is buffeted in the later acts after he has succeeded
in escaping from the knife. It is true that one situation seems to follow the other naturally and logically,
when certain premises are granted, for Mr. Mackaye
has employed his craft as a playwright with great
cunning and dexterity ; but the succession of dangers
and sufferings is prolonged to a point where sympathy
and interest are threatened with exhaustion, and the
spectator is no longer capable of astonishment or
emotion. It was for this reason, not because of any
actual falling off in the quality of the play or the performance, that the first two acts, while the imagination of the audience was yet unsated, made the deepest
impression on Saturday night. The device by which
Kauvar is induced to sign a blank warrant to be employed against his wife and her father, the two persons
of all others whom he was striving to shield from
arrest, is terribly shallow and improbable (it would

have been much better to let the villain forge the
whole paper) ; but the warrant once being issued,
the situations which grow out of it are strongly dramatic, and the climax, when the man who is risking
his life and deliberately wrecking his happiness for
the sake of the woman he loves is apparently con-
victed of the most cowardly and selfish treachery towards her, is cleverly conceived and admirably worked
out. There are several stirring passages in the second
act also, where the scene is laid in the Prison of the
Conciergerie adjoining the revolutionary tribunal, and
the prisoners are conducted to and from the fatal
court-room amid the savage cries of the unseen mob.
All this is well imagined and really impressive, and
the final tableau, where *Kauvar* is torn almost from
the arms of his wife to take his place in the tumbril
of the condemned, is another powerful climax ; but
the hackneyed expedient of an exchange of uniforms,
adopted with fairly good effect in this instance (difficult of belief as the situation is), certainly ought not
to have been used again in the fourth act, where it
suggests poverty of invention. Again, it is clearly in
the nature of anti-climax that *Kauvar*, after going to
the guillotine in the place of his unconscious father-
in-law, and escaping, should be willing to incur the
same peril once more, at the moment when there was
a chance of reunion with his wife ; but this is not the
only place where the author has refused to permit
considerations of this kind to stand in the way of a
situation. The third striking scene is at the end of
the third act, when the heroine, having learned of her
husband's devotion and the villain's treachery, pro-

claims her marriage, which has hitherto been secret, renounces her father and her false lover, and declares that she will henceforth cast in her lot with the people to whom her husband belonged. The situation here is not only very strong dramatically, but is original as well, and it was received on Saturday night with loud and prolonged applause. The scene in the final act, when *Kauvar*, playing the part of prisoner in the uniform of the royalist general whom he has helped to escape, and pledged to silence for an hour, holds his peace and conceals his identity, while his idolized wife is undergoing the deadliest of insults at the hands of a mob, is overwrought and unnatural. The man who would respect a sentimental obligation in such a case would be a good deal less than human. On the other hand, it is asking a good deal of credulity to assume that a mob inflamed with blood and passion would yield instant obedience to a man whose condition was presumptive proof of his treachery to their cause. It was necessary, however, at that juncture to end the play happily and in a hurry.

The piece is well acted and admirably mounted. The management of the mob is especially worthy of commendation. The irruption of the *Sans-culottes* into the grand hall of the Château Delaroche, and the destruction of the hangings and furniture, is one of the most realistic and picturesque scenes ever witnessed upon the local stage. It is extremely effective both in action and colour, and shows a great advance upon the ordinary slovenly methods of stage management. *Kauvar's* vision of the guillotine, in the first

K

act, with the dripping head in the hands of the executioner, and the savage crowd about the guillotine, is a tableau of horrible significance, and when the curtain fell upon the spectacle of the headsman's assistants placing the seemingly senseless form of Miss Annie Robe in readiness for the knife, the liveliest emotion was evinced by many of the spectators. The vision was greeted with uproarious applause, and was certainly an extraordinary, if rather ghastly, illusion. Mr. Joseph Haworth appeared as *Kauvar*, and enacted it with great and sustained melodramatic intensity. There was more of lung power than true emotional depth in his performance, but in a piece of this sort, in which probabilities are set at defiance, a little exaggeration is pardonable, and his impersonation is always picturesque and forcible, very sincere and manly, with many touches of simple pathos and some fine outbreaks of passion. Miss Robe made a great hit in her strong scene in the third act, when she defies father and betrothed, and rushes away to join the mob. The vigour of her declamation and the boldness and decision of her gesture revealed a greater amount of dramatic power than she has ever exhibited before, and were rewarded by a veritable storm of applause. The triumph was chiefly physical, but undoubtedly marked an upward step in her career. Mr. Lackaye played the villain with much emphasis, Mr. Edwin Varrey was dignified and correct as the persecuted *Duke*, and Mr. G. D. Fawcett gave a very vigorous sketch of the worst type of French ruffianism, with a touch of tigerish savagery in it. Mr. Leslie Allen, as a bluff old soldier, had

some unlucky lines to speak, but did well nevertheless, and the minor characters were all adequately
filled.   The representation, indeed, was far above the
common level in every way, and showed care and
intelligence everywhere.   The weakest point is the
comedy.   Mr. Mackaye's humour is apt to be rather
solemn, but he has never evolved anything quite so
dreary as his comic couple in " Paul Kauvar."   But
it is not fair to end with an expression of dissatisfac-
tion, for he has written a play which is full of pith
and fancy, in spite of its exaggerations and improbabilities, and in it extends assurance that he will do
better still by-and-by.

J. Ranken Towse.

WALL STREET ON THE STAGE.

["THE HENRIETTA."]

ONE of the most pronounced successes of 1887-88 was Mr. Bronson Howard's comedy, in four acts, "The Henrietta." It was brought out early in the season by the comedians, Robson and Crane, at the Union Square Theatre, New York; enjoyed a run of several months there, and subsequently repeated its original success in each of the cities of Philadelphia, Boston, and Chicago. The piece deals with the Wall Street and the social side of New York life. The plot carries us along with the daily life of the family of *Nicholas Vanalstyne*, the leader of the street, who is engaged, among other enterprises, in "booming" the stock of the Henrietta mine. His son, *Nicholas Vanalstyne Junior*, the father's confidential and trusted associate, is secretly plotting against his father and trying to ruin him, that he himself may become "the King of Wall Street." A younger son, *Bertie*, a good-hearted, simple-minded fellow of genus "dude," comes to the help of the financier at the critical moment, and saves him from ruin. The mental and physical strain caused by the failure of his plans, and the disclosure of his unfilial perfidy, is too much for the elder son, who drops

dead from heart disease. *Bertie* having discovered
that the secret of the stock-market lies in the toss up
of a coin, becomes a successful speculator, and is
duly recognized as a young Napoleon of finance.
Associated with this main thread of plot are minor
incidents. *Bertie* and *Agnes Lockwood*, a sister-in-law
of *Nicholas Junior*, are in love with each other, but are
for a time estranged by reason of *Bertie* magnanimously
bearing the burden of a *mésalliance* of his brother's
that that wily individual has foisted upon his younger
relative. *Dr. Parke Wainright* is in love with *Rose*,
the wife of *Nicholas Junior*, and, after she becomes a
widow, wins her. *Mrs. Cornelia Opdyke*, a wealthy
widow, is sought in marriage by the *Rev. Dr. Murray
Hilton*, a worldly-minded, unspiritual, Pecksniffian
parson, who has an eye only to the lady's wealth ;
and *Nicholas Senior*, being also determined to marry
the widow, wrecks a railroad in order to ruin both
the parson and the lady, and thus drive away his
rival. *Lady Mary Trelauney*, daughter of old
Vanalstyne, and her husband, *Lord Arthur*, figure in
the story, and there are complications arising from
the confusion and misjudgments that the existence or
supposed existence of a mine, a ballet-dancer, a
Kentucky racing filly and a female speculator, all
known by the name " Henrietta," naturally engender,
especially in the minds of the ladies of the household.

We have so often been invited to regale ourselves
intellectually with the great American comedy only
to find in the end that we have been seated at a
Barmecide feast, that we may well be pardoned a

certain amount of incredulity when the invitations
are again and again repeated. Although, with the
grace of Shacabac, we may courteously refrain from
showing our disappointment, yet we never feel quite
certain that, as in his case, the real banquet is ever
destined to follow. In fact, so far as our home stage
is concerned, the writing of pure comedy is a lost art,
or rather perhaps a neglected art, for we have really
never had much of it to lose ; at any rate, it is certainly
not now the vogue. Of excellent material in contemporary life for this purpose there is an abundance;
but the moment that the dramatic writer essays to
transport it, he gently slides off his log, and amiably
flounders about in the soiled waters of farce and burlesque. The prevailing taste of the day for spangles
and tights, roystering horse-play and drawing-room
acrobatics of course influences to this result. With
the demand comes the supply : along this road there
lies for the dramatic carpenter a certain kind of
popularity and much financial success, and conse-
quently many there be who walk therein. Now
farce, burlesque, extravaganza and all their ilk have
a proper place on the stage—and a pretty large place
they seem to occupy just now—but they are not the
highest forms of expression in dramatic art, nor are
they worthy the efforts of the dramatist who is
capable of better things ; certainly they must not be
set before us as a comedy, no heed whence their
origin.

This, then, must be our quarrel with "The Henrietta." The piece has been exploited as a comedy,
which it is not ; and it is a concession to a certain

public taste in matters theatrical that can by no
courtesy of phraseology be set down as either elevated or elevating.   We surely had a right to expect
something better than this from the author of " Old
Love Letters " and " The Banker's Daughter," and
hence perhaps to a considerable degree our disappointment.   The piece is not worthy the talent of
Mr. Howard, and we feel all the way through that it
is merely a clever piece of workmanship without any
seriousness of purpose behind it.   By the box-office
standard the play is unimpeachable ; but that must
not blind us to the truth regarding it as a work of
art.   " The Tin Soldier " and " The Rag Baby " have
the same argument behind them, and really when you
come to consider it carefully, the difference between
those plays and " The Henrietta " is one of degree
only and not of class.   " The Henrietta " is superior
to " The Rag Baby," inasmuch as Mr. Howard is a
superior workman to Mr. Hoyt—more refined and
more artistic, and with more of the pure literary instinct : that is all.   Mr. Hoyt raises a laugh by
making his porter tumble downstairs with a trunk ;
Mr. Howard achieves the same result by making one
of his ladies sit down abruptly on the floor when she
is expecting to fall gracefully into the arms of the
wooing stockbroker.   Instances of comparison might
be multiplied, but that will suffice.

On the whole, what we must deplore in the play as
a work of art, and in the characterizations of its
people, is the extravagance and unnaturalness that
distinguish it and them.   Comedy does not mean
unnaturalness.   On the contrary, the chief charm of

the old comedies is that their people, even while they
make us laugh at themselves, always act and talk
just as we imagine such people should act and talk.
Mr. Howard's people act and talk just as such people
never would act and talk. They are types—that
is, the men are, for the women are merely lay-figures
of familiar composition—but they are types exaggerated and distorted out of nearly all semblance to
harmonious consistency with themselves. Exceptions
must be made to *Bertie* and *Lord Arthur*, who, in
spite of the fact that they are gross caricatures, are
at least consistently and logically developed.

But with all its faults it may not be denied that
"The Henrietta" is intensely interesting. The underlying idea is well conceived, the plot is clearly
worked out, the incidents and the situations are
effective, and there is much clever dialogue in it.
The fine lines, the delicate touches, the gentle wit
that belong to comedy pure and simple, are absent
to be sure : in their stead we have a breadth of
delineation, an extravagance of caricature, some vulgarity and much true humour. The best part of the
dialogue is put into the mouths of *Bertie* and *Lord
Arthur*, and there is keen satire in many of their
speeches—a satire that has both force and point to
it, although it is to be feared that with the audience
the lesson of the satire is lost in the overpowering
humour of the lines. On the whole, then, while
withholding praise from the play as a worthy piece
of dramatic art, we may recognize it as entertaining
in its way, cleverly holding up as it does the mirror
to certain foibles of contemporaneous life, and in-

spiring for the most part to wholesome merriment and abundant even if unintellectual exhilaration of spirit.

This was the cast of the play :—

Nicholas Vanalstyne	. . .	Mr. Wm. H. Crane
Dr. Parke Wainwright	. . .	Mr. H. J. Lethcourt
Nicholas Vanalstyne, Jr.	. . .	Mr. Charles Kent
Bertie Vanalstyne	. . .	Mr. Stuart Robson
Lord Arthur Trelauney	. . .	Mr. Lorimer Stoddard
Rev. Dr. Murray Hilton	. . .	Mr. Frank Tannehill, Jr.
Watson Flint	. . . .	Mr. Henry Bergman
Musgrave	. . . . .	Mr. Louis Carpenter
Mrs. Cornelia Opdyke	. . .	Miss Selena Fetter
Rose Vanalstyne	. . ' .	Miss Sibyl Johnstone
Agnes Lockwood	. . . .	Miss Jessie Storey
Lady Mary Trelauney	. . .	Miss May Waldron

Mr. Crane's impersonation was notable for its vigour, its brusqueness of style and its unctuous humor. Necessarily it had the blemishes of the author's conception. At no time did the antagonistic characteristics of the *rôle* quite harmoniously blend into a well-balanced whole : the line of demarcation was always plainly to be seen, and you could scarcely reconcile the cold-blooded wrecker of railroads with the good-humoured schemer against the parson and the farcically behaving lover. Such a character might be, but here its parts did not hang together well. But in the delineation of its several moods Mr. Crane was admirable, acting with a wholesomeness of spirit, a breeziness of air, and a tenderness of sympathetic feeling that was as inspiriting as it was artistic. Mr. Robson's impersonation of the stupid, innocent, good-hearted idler who cannot distinguish between the operations of Wall Street and the play of the gaming-table ; who delights in *outré* dress ; who with others of his ilk spends his time in "just staying at the Club, each of us thinking that the other is a devil of a fellow—but he isn't ;" who can patiently bear the burden of his brother's wickedness—the impersonation was in the artist's best vein, deliciously droll in its humorous moments, and yet informed by much of dramatic feeling and power in its serious passages. Mr. Stoddard's *Lord Arthur* was intelligently done. In make-up, in gait, in languid air, in drawling, listless speech, he caricatured the English swell cleverly and with discriminating touch. The *Rev. Dr. Murray Hilton* of Mr. Tannehill was a vivid characterization very clearly and forcibly presented. Of the remaining members of the cast it will be sufficient to say that they filled their respective *rôles* sufficiently well, and that they acted together in a manner that secured for the play an unusually smooth, well-balanced and artistic presentation.

LYMAN H. WEEKS.

"LA TOSCA."

THE particular feature of Miss Fanny Davenport's season was the production of M. Victorien Sardou's new play, " La Tosca," at the opening of the New Broadway Theatre in New York, on Saturday evening, March 3rd, 1888. After a fairly successful engagement in New York—made so, perhaps, by the unnecessary agitation regarding the morality of the play raised by certain newspapers—Miss Davenport started upon a tour in the far West, to San Francisco, Portland and other places, which extended well into the summer. Previous to the production of " La Tosca " Miss Davenport had given in various cities performances of " Fédora " and other well-known pieces in her repertory.

The theme upon which M. Sardou has worked in " La Tosca " is no doubt known to the readers of this volume. It is simply a story of fiendish cruelty and lust, of which *Scarpia*, quite as much as *Floria Tosca* herself, is the central figure. Briefly *La Tosca* is a singer, a passionate, petulant woman—inordinately jealous, as all such women are—violently in love with a young painter, *Mario Cararadossi*. The scene of the play, by the way, is Rome in 1800, and a good many political allusions aid in giving it a rather revolutionary atmosphere. The first act is devoted to a long explanatory dialogue between the painter, at work in St. Andrew's Church upon a fresco, and *Cesare Angellotti*, a fugitive from a Roman prison. *Mario* arranges to aid *Angellotti's* escape by concealing him for a while in his own villa at Frascati. While they are still talking, *La Tosca* comes to the door of the chapel; the fugitive conceals himself and the singer is admitted. She has heard voices while waiting, and *Mario* is put to it to allay her jealous fears in consequence. When finally she goes, *Angellotti* finds the opportunity to make his escape with *Mario* by dressing himself in woman's clothes obtained from his sister, the *Marquise Altavanti*. Unfortunately, he leaves a fan behind, which *Scarpia*, entering the church in pursuit, is fortunate enough to find. With this he seeks *La Tosca* at the Farnese Palace, where the next act opens, and arouses in her uncontrollable suspicions of *Mario's* fidelity. The third act, the most highly dramatic and the most hideous of all, comes off at the painter's villa. *La Tosca* bursts in upon him, jealous, passionate, impetuous, imperious. She shows him the fan, and demands to see the *Marquise*. When she learns the truth, she realizes her folly; worse, she remembers that *Scarpia* has followed her, and is likely to discover the truth as well as she. *Scarpia* arrives; *Mario* is conducted to another room and tortured, and *La Tosca* is told that the only way she can deliver her lover from his horrible agony is by revealing *Angellotti's* hiding-place. While she hesitates, *Mario's* screams and groans ring in her ears; she can make but one choice —to reveal the secret which *Mario* has bidden her keep. This, as we have already indicated, is at once the most hideous and most impressive scene in the play. Even *Scarpia's* insulting proposals to *La Tosca* in the next act, her seeming consent to them as the only price that he will accept for her lover's life, and her deliverance of herself from his loathed embrace by plunging a knife in his throat—even these moments of horror are less torturing to the imagination of the spectator than the sickening agonies of the Inquisition. And the final act in the prison, where *Mario* is led away to execution secure in *La Tosca's* assurance that his escape has been provided for by *Scarpia*, and the last scene, in which the woman, learning how *Scarpia's* last deed was one of deception, and how her lover is dead despite that mortal fiend's assurances, plunges from the parapet into the river beneath, are both altogether less vivid in their display of the hellish potency of evil than the two fiery intervals of passion which have preceded them.

To say that such a play as this is powerful is merely to give utterance to a commonplace of criticism. But as a work of art "La Tosca" will not bear a moment's comparison, one need not say with the great tragedies of literature, but even with the previous efforts of M. Sardou himself to sound the heights and depths of human emotion. Its strength lies almost wholly in its ingenuity of repulsiveness and horror. The crimes portrayed are rather those of devils than of men. There is not a single scene in the piece that deserves comparison for its artistic nearness to humanity with the two great scenes of "Fédora." Its force is that of dramatic hysterics rather than artistic power. M. Sardou appears to be

emulating some of the minor Elizabethan dramatists
in accumulating horrors which merely appal the outward senses, and do not in the least engage the imagination. His model is " The Revenger's Tragedy "
of Cyril Tourneur rather than Shakspere's " Othello."
His passion is rapidly degenerating from the dignity
of genuine tragedy to the raving billingsgate of a
fishwife. A great deal of gabble has been going on,
as we have already said, about the immorality of " La
Tosca." But it is absurd to call the play immoral,
unless one is prepared to accept Mr. Podsnap's young
person as representing the only proper critical
standard. " La Tosca " is certainly not a play for
that ingenious observer to see or hear without a blush ;
but it is not immoral, if we mean by that word (and
what other meaning is possible ?) that the effect upon
the adult spectator is to make immorality pleasant
and attractive. It is hideous, repulsive, possibly even
debasing ; but it is absurd to say that no decent
person can attend a performance of it without harm.
It would be quite within the bounds of moderation,
however, to say that no decent person can possibly be
benefited by so inartistic, so coarse and so revolting
a portraiture of the very worst side of human nature.

As every one knows, " La Tosca " was written for
Mdme. Bernhardt, and was produced by her at the
Porte St. Martin Theatre in Paris last November.
Miss Fanny Davenport's methods are so different to
those of the French artist that one can hardly imagine
from the performance in New York what the original
production can have been. It is certain that Miss
Davenport's Italian singer has the Saxon temperament,

and that her varying moods of passion lack almost entirely the ardent, impetuous and slightly sinuous quality which M. Sardou must have intended should belong to them. In the lighter phases of the first two acts, indeed, Miss Davenport was singularly ineffective; for one thing, her caprice seemed too deliberately studied. In the following scenes she was immensely more satisfactory. Never reaching, perhaps, the very highest point of tragic power, never permeating the mind of the spectator with the sense of dramatic intensity, there were yet passages in which the fitful fire of the undoubted genius which underlies Miss Davenport's work flashed out with brilliant effect. The method was bad and the achievement, regarded as a whole, was unsuccessful; but here and there were touches which deserved the heartiest commendation. One such touch, perhaps the most vivid, is the moment in the third act when *La Tosca* falls on her knees and begs *Scarpia* for time to think before she betrays *Angellotti* to save her lover from torture. So far as the supporting company goes, silence is scant charity. Mr. McDowell was weak and ineffective as *Mario*, and Mr. Mordaunt—though at times not altogether unimpressive in his portraiture of sensuality and brutality—could hardly have done worse with the powerful part of *Scarpia* if he had set about burlesquing it. The scenery was beautiful and elaborate, and the accessories of the performance, costumes, furnishings, organ, choir boys, &c., were provided with a lavish hand.

EDITOR.

PART III.

MDME. JANAUSCHEK.

NOT the least interesting and important of the theatrical events of the season of 1887-88 was the appearance of that greatest of living tragic actresses, Mdme. Janauschek, at the Boston Museum, with the regular company of that house. Previous to that event she had played during a part of the season in Western cities and in Philadelphia and Brooklyn; but the three weeks of her engagement in Boston, which began April 16th and ended May 5th, formed by far the most notable part of her season. For two weeks she appeared as *Meg Merrilies*, an impersonation which she first took up only a year ago, and in which her great reputation as an artist of wonderful force and originality was increased, if that were possible; for the third week she devoted herself to " Bleak House," and to the dual impersonation in that play which is perhaps the most vivid and widely-contrasted piece of acting on the modern stage, with the exception of Saturday evening, when she appeared as *Lady Macbeth* at a testimonial performance in her honour. This occasion was a most remarkable one. The theatre was crowded from pit to dome by an audience of the highest intellectual and social character. The distinguished artist was very warmly received, and was called again and again before the curtain. At the end of her final scene she was brought out three times, and finally was compelled to speak a few words of farewell to her hearers. "I will not give myself the pain of saying good-bye," she said; "I will only ask you to remember me and my acting." These words must have emphasized the general feeling of regret which her magnificent impersonation of *Lady Macbeth* aroused—regret that it was a single performance and possibly the last which Mdme. Janauschek would ever give, at least in America. Yet it must have been a pleasure to every one in the house, as well, to feel that her farewell had been in every way a memorable one. The public approval which the announcement of a testimonial to her had won from men of distinction was a tribute to which the character of the audience on Saturday evening gave added weight. We do not forget even the brilliant series of performances given by Mr. Booth and by Mr. Irving here this winter when we say that the production of "Macbeth," in which Mdme. Janauschek was the chief figure, fairly deserves to be recorded as the most important single event of the entire season. How this great artist impresses the most cultivated lovers of the stage the following expression of opinion from one of the distinguished men who signed the public letter to her, to which allusion has already been made, may serve to illustrate. "I have a great admiration and respect," this competent critic writes, "for Mdme. Janauschek's career and art. We all owe her much, for her influence on acting in this country has been a fine one. She is one of the few actors I have seen in my time who have thoroughly known how to unite the most intense truth of feeling with nobleness of form and perfect training; to infuse into the simplicity, exactitude and moderation of the realistic school the divine fire of genius. I shall always look back on some of the occasions on which I have seen her as among those which afforded my fullest glimpses of the possible greatness of the stage." To this just and adequate tribute the present writer cannot hope to add anything of value. Besides, this is neither the time nor the place for a careful and elaborate estimate of the quality of Mdme. Janauschek's genius. It is only in order here to comment with as much brevity as is possible upon three impersonations, all of which are more or less known to theatre-goers.

There is no need now to dwell upon the fact that Mdme. Janauschek's impersonation of *Lady Macbeth* is without doubt or qualification a work of absolute genius which can only be described as incomparable. Like her *Medea* and her *Brunhild*, which have become an inseparable part of the glories of the modern stage, it is resistless in its tragic force and flawless in its tragic grandeur. From the impressive instant of her entrance upon the scene, through all the intense and terrible crises of emotion and passion which fill up the measure of her dramatic life to the last awful moments of distraction and remorse, she dominates the shuddering imagination of the spectator as few other artists since Mrs. Siddons have dominated it. The nature of acting is such that comparison is difficult if not impossible ; but the closest readers of the history of the stage will find no one whom they would be willing to admit could have surpassed Mdme. Janauschek in that force and that grandeur which, as we have indicated, are the primary qualities of her genius. In the words of an excellent judge of acting, such characterizations as her *Lady Macbeth* give one a new sense of the possibilities of dramatic art. This, it is true, is very extravagant praise ; but we do not fancy that any critic who will candidly compare Mdme. Janauschek's acting in this part with anything else of the sort that he has ever seen will consider it excessive. Certainly no other *Lady Macbeth* could so fully realize the highest conception of the thoughtful student of Shakspere. It is that "high-strung nervous energy," as Professor Dowden calls it, which carries through the ghastly tragedy of *Duncan's* murder. The cowardly irresolution, the vague imaginative remorse in which her husband loses his self-control, is not possible to her firm and courageous nature. What Von Schlegel says of the play itself that "since the ' Eumenides ' of Æschylus nothing so grand and terrible has ever been written "— can easily be applied to the character from which its deadly action springs. And it is something of this old Greek sublimity that fills Mdme. Janauschek's impersonation. Perhaps there is idealization here ; but then a *Lady Macbeth* who was not idealized would obviously be a creature of melodrama rather than of tragedy. The play itself is translated by the pure force of poetry and dramatic invention above the grooves of ordinary existence ; to borrow from Von Schlegel once more, "it is as if the drags were taken from the wheels of time, and they rolled along without interruption in their descent." The weird sisters embody the irony of fate ; but in the foreground are the two guilty creatures whose own natures are their betrayers and of whom the woman is by far the greater and the more magnificent criminal. To portray such a woman is at once the most serious and the highest task to which an artist can dedicate her powers. Mdme. Janauschek does this with a splendour and fulness of creative energy which beggar praise.

Of the individual points of Mdme. Janauschek's impersonation we wish that we had here the opportunity to give some adequate consideration ; but only a few of the more significant of these can be discussed within the limits of a notice like this. It should be said at the outset that Mdme. Janauschek is singularly well fitted personally for the part. Her fine and strong face can express that temperamental force and power to awe which make the ideal of majesty ; and in every step and gesture there is both strength and royalty. Mrs. Siddons's belief that *Lady Macbeth* was a slight woman, a nervous blonde, will hardly bear serious examination ; her mastery of her husband's weaker nature was not the outcome of fitful energy but of native imperiousness. From the moment of Mdme. Janauschek's appearance upon the stage—be it observed in passing that she is obviously reading for a second or third time her husband's letter, and is not, as Mdme. Ristori absurdly supposed, ignorant of its contents—this imperiousness becomes a part of the consciousness of the spectator ; no one can doubt the meaning of her promise—

> Glamis thou art and Cawdor, and shalt be
> What thou art promised.

Mdme. Janauschek's utterance of these words, indeed, sets the keynote of her impersonation. Each corporal agent is hereafter bent up to the terrible feat at which her husband sickens and recoils. This fact is emphasized by the awful appeal to the "spirits that tend on mortal thoughts," and again by the words, into which Mdme. Janauschek puts a malicious significance which fairly sets the blood tingling, "He that's coming must be provided for." And again in the scene with her husband just before the murder the same relentless energy in its most impressive manifestation takes the imagination captive. We must notice in passing that Mdme. Janauschek gives the two much-disputed words, "We fail," the only really significant meaning which they can possibly possess. She does not make of them a question or an explanation ; they are simply an admission of the possibility of failure which the instant appeal to *Macbeth* to screw his courage to the sticking-point contemptuously dismisses. But nothing in the impersonation is more impressive and convincing in its fidelity to nature than the scene in the courtyard. Too much a woman not to feel the horror of the time, the compunctious visitings of nature from which *Lady Macbeth* has prayed to be delivered—and one of these is exquisitely indicated by Mdme. Janauschek as she recalls with sudden tenderness the King's resemblance to her father—fail nevertheless to shake her from her fell purpose. Yet again the woman's nature (for she cannot be all unsexed) is indicated

with a beautiful and vivid insight by the sudden gesture of disgust with which she turns away from the
bloody daggers. In another moment her scornful and
terrible exclamation—

> Infirm of purpose !
> Give me the daggers ; the sleeping and the dead
> Are but as pictures—

restores the malevolent and implacable spirit of evil.
But that spirit is exhausted in this one stroke : and
after that, *Lady Macbeth*, unlike her husband, sinks
no deeper into the abyss of crime, except as the " limed
soul, that struggling to be free," is more involved. In
the banquet scene all the potency of her character is
directed to sustaining the burden under which her
husband sinks; and here Mdme. Janauschek's representation of the real force and strength of the woman is
something never to be forgotten. With comparatively few words, but with a royalty of self-control
that never falters, she moves among the guests with
apparent unconcern and endeavours to restore her
husband's self possession. And the weary gesture
with which she bows her head over her husband as the
curtain falls only augments the impression of purely
tragic intensity which the moment conveys. In the
final glimpse of *Lady Macbeth* which the dramatist
gives us, where at last the sting of remorse has pene-
trated the guilty woman's soul, so that in her sleeping
hours she lives the awful past over again, Mdme.
Janauschek portrays the mingled terror and pathos of
absolute hopelessness and despair in a way that we
have never seen it portrayed before. " There can-

not be a sting in death more sharp" than the pang
which the tortured mind of this woman undergoes in
life. And all the awe and pity of her horror and
remorse breathe through the whispered words which
are the last we hear her speak.

It is only little more than a year now since Mdme.
Janauschek first undertook to play *Meg Merrilies.*
Since Charlotte Cushman, with whose name the part
had become peculiarly identified, no one had ventured
to attempt to embody upon the stage the potent sibyl
of Scott's imagination. It is easy, perhaps, to be
grotesque ; it is comparatively easy, given a certain
temperament, to be tragic ; but how to be both grotesque and tragic and never to sacrifice one quality
to another apparently its direct opposite is something
which even genius itself might easily confess its in-
ability to undertake. For nothing is clearer than the
fact that the strange being who really dominates
Scott's novel is something more than a half-crazed
gipsy. Yet if we are to accept her as a witch she is
plainly as far removed from the broomstick creatures
of tradition as are the weird sisters of " Macbeth "
themselves. To make such a character as this natural
and human and intelligible enough to appeal to the
imagination of the spectator is, as has been indicated,
no slight problem. Miss Cushman was inspiring
enough as the sibyl ; but she failed to embody with
distinctness the woman. She was grotesque ; but
(speaking under the possibility of being corrected by
those who have a clearer impression of her impersonation) she was not tragic. It is upon this side of the

characterization, where she failed, that Mdme. Janauschek succeeds. This *Meg Merrilies* of her creation is
not only picturesquely impressive ; she is deeply and
pathetically human. The figure of the old gipsy,
thus conceived, imparts to the somewhat tawdry play
the dignity of serious drama. From the moment she
appears, flinging aside the curtains of her tent with
an imperious gesture, she dominates the stage and
holds the admiration and sympathy of the spectator.
In all her half-crazed utterances there is a potent
charm that holds the imagination captive. First of
all, old and haggard and broken as she is, she is a
queen over the wild tribe with whom she lives. The
bolder spirits affect to scorn her, and even to believe
that her wits and strength are failing ; but her cry
when *Harry Bertram's* life is at stake—" Gipsies, strike
not at your peril !" disperses the conspirators like
chaff before the wind. Hardly anything in one's
recollections of the stage can be more vivid, we fancy,
than the impression made by Mdme. Janauschek's
appearance on the rocks above the glen at this crisis
in the young heir's fate. But even more singular in
its appeal to the emotion of the spectator is the exquisite pathos of her dying words with the youth for
whom she has suffered so much ; even more than in
the scenes of greater dramatic strength is the genius
of the artist clearly displayed.

Of Mdme. Janauschek's wonderful dual impersonation in " Bleak House " there is no need now to speak.
It is too familiar to theatre-goers to call for discussion
in a volume which deals only with what is new to the
stage. But even the repetition in a given season of

so transcendent a work of genius as these distinctly differentiated rôles—each a masterpiece in its way and each performed with unabated force and finish through a play of great length and in many differing phases —deserves a word of honest and hearty acknowledgment in passing. It would be difficult to say whether *Lady Dedlock* or *Hortense* is the more admirable impersonation. The latter is the more vivid and picturesque, undoubtedly, and in one or two passionate moments more expressive in the exhibition of pure mimetic genius. That final scene with *Bucket*, for instance, is not easily to be paralleled in its way. *Lady Dedlock*, on the other hand, with all the strangely latent power for good or evil which makes her so singularly interesting, is not an incarnation of female devilry, like her maid, and therefore her success with an audience does not depend so much upon a series of brilliant strokes as upon the sustained strength and dignity of the characterization. It is precisely in these qualities, however, that success is often most difficult; and this consideration makes us unwilling to admit that either part of this magnificent achievement of Mdme. Janauschek's is inferior to the other. Perhaps we can best realize the real value of her *Lady Dedlock* by imagining how an actress trained in the melodramatic gymnastics of the modern school would play it.

EDITOR.

THE TWO TRAGEDIANS, BOOTH AND BARRETT.

WHEN the dramatic and business partnership of Edwin Booth with Lawrence Barrett was proposed, an opinion prevailed generally to the effect that the association was incongruous and would end in unsatisfactory if not disastrous results. But the events of the season have not borne out this expectation ; on the contrary, there has been a pecuniary advantage for the two actors as well as an estimable gain for the theatre-going public.

The union has brought into the relationship of strong support and contrast the erratic ease of nonchalant genius and the steady formalism of industrious talent, and so given to the public something well worth the having which otherwise could not have been had.

Mr. James E. Murdoch, so long the friend and professional associate of the elder Booth, is my authority for saying that Edwin Booth's father replied to him, when he offered to give the promising lad some special training : "No, no, Teddy will never learn anything by teaching—he will only learn through his eyes and ears." Certainly Mr. Booth has never shown himself as a creator of new impersonations during all his long and influential career, and I do not recall as I write any drama in his repertory except "The Fool's Revenge" which has not come down to him from his father, or in which he does not reflect the character imparted to his rôle by that father, with such modifications as his native disposition and the gradual growth of years have brought to it. A student and a scholar in a certain closet fashion, and necessarily enlarging his scope and his power by the nightly exercise of his art, he has not been willing to bear the drudgery of hard work either upon his parts or upon those of the persons by whom he was surrounded and supported—if that environment with which he has too often evidently contented himself deserve the name of support. One great venture, indeed, did have the aid of his name, his money and his own participation; but it may be questioned if he contributed more than these, or gave time and strength to the active direction of the stage which cost him so dearly. His nature has seemed amply satisfied if it had an opportunity of saying its own words, casting its own glances and vivifying its own actions, without caring whether there were adequate cause or response in the mimic world about it. It has been a strange compound of enthusiasm and indifferentism, of dull but consuming flame and sluggish ice.

Mr. Barrett, on the other hand, has been a worker. Nothing that his hand or head could find to do has been beneath his attention or has been neglectfully treated. Beginning with only so much capital in talent as seemed adequate for the position of a leading man in the ordinary stock companies of twenty or thirty years ago, his restless, ambitious, sincere,

energetic and untiring disposition has given him from
year to year the best fruits of his natural gift, and their
assiduous cultivation. Not always wise in the means
he has chosen for his development, and ignoring others
which would have been invaluable, as their want has
detracted from the worth of his work, he has had purpose, pride and persistency, not alone for himself, but
for the whole dramatic art so far as it was given him
to be its exponent or its fosterer. Never satisfied
with the present and still less willing to be bound to
the past, he has demanded of the author new plays,
of the painter and the draper scenes and costumes
not only becoming but true, and he has exacted of
his companies severe and intelligent devotion to the
preparation in which he was ready and desirous to
participate and to lead.

What then, in brief, does the co-operation of these
two tragedians provide? It provides for Mr. Booth a
trained and competent support, headed by his coad-
jutor, and it brings to their joint work a certain
element of intrinsic force and freedom which a drama
enacted without Mr. Booth's assistance could not
have. It provides for the proper embodiment of passionate and sentimental parts by the man who has
always depended on the natural graces of his voice
and person, and it supplies for such other parts as can
be sufficiently enlivened by the efforts of intellect and
scholarship their true characterization. It enables
the wholesale admirers of Mr. Booth to see for themselves what his manner of life as an actor has missed,
as it enables those who have without reflection preferred Mr. Barrett to realize what his rigid, artificial

and often erroneous elocution is when compared with
the balanced rhythm of Mr. Booth's delivery. It has
helped the friends of each to know and appreciate
the other, and it has offered a merely personal attraction so strong that the public has gone eagerly to
performances of the greatest plays, finding them con-
scientiously and carefully produced and therefore
deriving all the mental and moral good which the
classic stage is capable of conveying.

The two tragedians occupied the Boston Theatre
for a fortnight, beginning on the 12th of December,
1887. Their whole engagement was devoted to
Shakspere, and the constant affluence of patronage,
which filled the house at advanced prices, was yet
another proof that when the master's tragedies are
honourably and sympathetically presented, there will
be an ample support in money as well as in kindly
feeling.

The first week was given up to " Julius Cæsar," in
which Mr. Barrett repeated his well-understood impersonation of *Cassius*, while Mr. Booth re-entered
into that of *Brutus*, the natural manners of the two
men, no less than their art, making the right contrast
plain to any eye. Mr. Barrett, without losing his
command of the nervous incisiveness befitting the
character, has advantageously modified his bearing
so as to bring *Cassius* nearer to *Brutus* and so make
the former's attitude more truly personal and less
declamatory and unfriendly.

During the second week the bill was changed frequently, and the distribution of the principal parts was
as follows :—" Lear " had Mr. Booth in the title-rôle

and Mr. Barrett for *Edgar;* Mr. Booth's *Macbeth* was
faced by Mr. Barrett's *Macduff;* in " The Merchant
of Venice," Mr. Booth was the *Shylock* and Mr.
Barrett the *Bassanio;* in "Othello," Mr. Barrett took
the part of the Moor, leaving *Iago* to Mr. Booth ;
while in " Hamlet " Mr. Barrett assumed *Laertes*, in
opposition to Mr. Booth's assumption of the Prince of
Denmark.

Now criticism and chronicle have not to set down
what one likes, but one coldly sees and impar-
tially weighs; and this being so, one cannot easily
avoid awarding the higher honours in art of these two
weeks to Mr. Barrett. I admit,—as I ever have admitted since the night when Edwin Booth came back
a grown man to Boston, and reintroduced himself
through his thrilling *Sir Giles Overreach,*—the potency
of his genius, the charm of his person, the music of
his voice, and the spell of his glance—all those inborn
advantages which in their union he received in greater
measure than any other tragedian of his time. I recognize, too, the less rich and varied natural equip-
ment of Mr. Barrett, his lack of elasticity in bearing
and the want of sweetness and equability in voice
and diction.

But I cannot help seeing that Mr. Barrett has
prized his endowment, and profited by it more than
Mr. Booth, and that he has not rested content with
anything less than the closest assimilation to his ideal
of character which has appeared possible to him.
That Mr. Booth should not now be always faithful to his text is to be regretted ; but it is also to be
forgiven. Exactitude of memory cannot be com-

manded, especially if one's organization be nervous and high strung, and one's disposition be somewhat moody. But that he persistently neglects the resources of his profession, so far as " making up" is concerned, and presents men of thirty with the face and the grizzling hair of fifty, is bad art and bad faith with the public. There would be as much sense in putting into "Othello " an *Iago* in top-boots as to put into the tragedy of Denmark a *Hamlet* past middle age. Such an ignoring of the " unities," of the action, and of the proper presentment of individual character, detracts alike from the pleasure and good of a play and from the credit to which even the greatest acting would otherwise be entitled.

In a word, in Mr. Booth one sees a glorious personality and great gifts drifting along as if by chance, the one declining without repair, and the others taking on that increment only which maturity and experience bring to every not inactive man, so long as he has not absolutely " declined into the vale of years." In Mr. Barrett, on the other hand, one sees energy, determination and intelligence, all exerted to hold every past gain and to make as much more as may be, and to fit idea, time, place and circumstance with correspondent illustration. One may enjoy Mr. Booth the more—I confess I often do—but one must give Mr. Barrett the greater credit as an honest and consistent professor of the art.

The mounting of the pieces was generally good— that of " Julius Cæsar," indeed, was almost spectacular—and but few mistakes were made, the only censurable one being the presentation of the body of the drowned *Ophelia*. The company, including no remarkable actors, yet did its work well, and gave evidence of careful training well remembered. Indeed, in some instances—especially in that of the leading lady, Miss Minna K. Gale—there was only too apparent the influence of Mr. Barrett, not only in prescribing the " business," which was all well enough, but also in dictating the delivery, which thus became an imitation, more or less caricatured, of the least estimable of his peculiarities in elocution. Miss Miriam O'Leary gave some of the smaller rôles with welcome naturalness, and the heavier parts were creditably taken by Miss Gertrude Kellogg and Miss Elizabeth Robins, while among the men ought to be noted Mr. John A. Lane, Mr. E. J. Buckley, who gave to *Marc Antony* a deal of crude power and not always wisely directed warmth, Mr. Owen Fawcett, who as the *First Citizen,* led energetically the numerous and hustling mob which modern realism insists upon intruding into the scenes in the Senate and the Forum.

HOWARD MALCOM TICKNOR.

.

M 2

MR. IRVING IN AMERICA.

MR. IRVING'S third season in America was confined to four cities, in each of which his success was remarkable. He began his engagement in New York at the Star Theatre, November 7th, 1887. Five weeks later he went to Philadelphia for a fortnight, and from there to Chicago, where he remained four weeks. On the 23rd of January, 1888, he came to Boston for another four weeks, returning again to New York on the 20th of February for five weeks more. His second season in that city ended on the 24th of March. Mr. Irving then sailed for England immediately, reappearing at his own theatre in April. Of his repertory during his American visit, "Faust" was the *pièce de résistance*, but "Olivia" was also given with general acceptation, and the more familiar plays, "Louis XI.," "The Lyons Mail," "The Merchant of Venice" and "The Bells" received a number of performances. Mr. Irving was also seen for the first time in America in "Jingle," a farce adapted from "The Pickwick Papers." Both he and Miss Terry were individually very successful, and other artists in the company also met with a favourable reception. Both plays and performances are discussed at some length in the following pages.

The history of Mr. Irving's production of "Faust" is so familiar to our readers that it need not be rehearsed at length here. It is worth while to remember that it first saw the light at the Lyceum Theatre, London, December 19th, 1885; that Mr. Conway was then the *Faust;* that the scene of the witches' kitchen was added November 15th, 1886; that the play then ran without interruption until June of last year, when it was alternated with other plays previous to Mr. Irving's departure for this country; and that it was first brought out in America at the Star Theatre, New York, November 7th, 1887.

To attempt to shape Goethe's work for the stage is a task which must naturally be only in part successful, at best; and the more closely Mr. Wills's work is studied, the more admirable from the purely dramatic point of view it appears to us to be. To the student of "Faust" in its original form it will of course be disappointing, but Mr. Wills has probably done as well as any one could do in selecting from the huge bulk of undigested material the passages which can be combined within reasonable limits to make a stage version of adequate but not exhaustive scope. The reader will bear in mind, of course, that we are speaking of his work from the dramatic rather than the literary point of view. As a piece of translation pure and simple the piece has many faults; nor has it preserved so nearly as one might properly wish the genuine poetic flavour of the original. To criticize it upon this score, however, would be rather profitless, as well as away from the purpose of the present notice. Briefly, then, if the play as arranged does not appeal so vividly to the imagination of the beholder as it might, if it now and then reaches melodramatic rather than purely tragic or pathetic levels, there is nevertheless enough to praise in its vigour, brilliancy and theatrical effectiveness.

There is at least one obvious excuse which may be made for Mr. Wills. The "Faust" of the Lyceum is largely an appeal more to the eye than to the intellect. No competent critic can possibly see it played from beginning to end without coming to this conclusion. Furthermore, most critics, we fancy, will be so thoroughly impressed with this fact that they will stand in danger of doing less than justice to the good sense and the good taste of the mechanical part of the production. There is an instinctive consciousness that the sublimity of the "Faust" legend, as Goethe left it, has been in some measure impaired and vulgarized. But as one looks less and less for the development of the merely scenic splendours and comes to study more carefully the sweep and movement of the play, the impression of its dignity and reality deepens and strengthens. One gets further and further away from grisly stage apparitions into the higher regions of the awful and tragic pathos of the story itself. One begins to lose sight of the demons and witches in following with hushed and breathless intentness the struggles of a weak human soul in the meshes of a potent and terrible fiend, and the ruin and rescue of an innocent and loving heart. Of course the scenic features of the play have an impressiveness of their own; but to our mind, brilliant as they are, they have been properly subordi-

nated to the dramatic interest of the narrative itself.
This aspect of Mr. Irving's production of " Faust " is
so fully and competently discussed by an accomplished critic elsewhere in this volume, that it need
not be dwelt upon here. We need only observe in
passing that the stage-setting of the pieces gives renewed testimony to Mr. Irving's singular ability as
a stage-manager, and that it is in every way noteworthy for its effectiveness and its artistic unity and
completeness The scenes in the witches' kitchen
and on the summit of the Brocken are simply marvellous, and the latter, in particular, is a triumph of
the resources of the modern stage in presenting the
most difficult pictures with well-nigh perfect illusion
to the eye of the spectator. The quieter scenes in
old Nürnberg are exquisitely done, and the exterior
and interior of the St. Lorenz-Kirche in the third act
deserve the heartiest commendation for their artistic
and poetic value. They reach that difficult point in
all scenic display—beauty without too much elaboration, and effectiveness without garish spectacular
glitter.

But the feature of the production around which
everything else revolves, and to which even every
outward and visible detail is properly subordinated,
is Mr. Irving's impersonation of *Mephistopheles.* It
is always dangerous to say of this or that creation of
any artist that it towers distinctly above his other
work ; it is impossible, indeed, that such an one should
be adequately represented even by his best. But it
is quite within proper critical bounds to say that
nothing else which Mr. Irving has done surpasses

his *Mephistopheles*, all things considered. *Mephisto-pheles* is so stupendous an embodiment of evil that one who portrays him with reasonable force and vividness need advance no further claim to the rank of a genuine artist. Mr Irving makes the fiend a sort of a rarified and sublimated *Iago*. He affects at times a careless jollity, a specious show of good-humour and good-nature. We are almost ready to see *Faust* clap him on the back and call him "honest *Mephistopheles*," in imitation of *Othello's* designation of his ancient. His raillery of the addle-pated soldiers in the St. Lorenz-Platz may fairly be compared with *Iago's* merriment over the clinking of the canikin. Not to push the parallel too far, he tempts *Faust* to the love of *Margaret* which is to be her ruin much as *Iago* instils into *Othello's* ear the jealousy which is to destroy *Desdemona*. But this merry devilry is only one side of Mr. Irving's creation. We find it in its most malign aspect in the scenes by the church in the third act, where he brings about the death of *Valentine* and where he usurps the priestly office to lure *Margaret* onward to the black abyss which he has opened beneath her feet. We find it in its most terrible aspect in the garden, where he flashes into a passion of anger and hatred that blinds the imagination of *Faust* with a glimpse of his hellish potency. We find it again in its most profound and awful aspect in the domination of the revelling spirits upon the summit of the Brocken. Here Mr. Irving's *Mephistopheles* is an incarnation of evil comparable with the *Lucifer* of Milton. Though fallen among the powers of darkness he cannot altogether forget his old station among the powers of light. As he stands against the cliff, with the baleful fiery light that always follows him full upon his face, there is both in attitude and expression a touch of something like pathos that is singularly poignant; there is · an awful sadness in the eyes that the satiric leer of one who revels in the force and potency of evil cannot altogether conceal. It is precisely this final touch that makes Mr. Irving's impersonation a really great one and fills its demonic energy and malice with a single flash of humanity and of poetic colour. And the pervading humour with which the actor invests the part, grimly satiric as it is, still further adds to its impressiveness on the purely human side. *Sancta simplicitas!* he exclaims when he finds that *Faust* has a conscience. "Where will she go when she dies, I wonder?" he asks after his good-night to *Martha*, adding quickly, "*I* won't have her!" It is this satiric and cynical force which gives Mr. Irving's impersonation a measure of completeness.

Miss Terry's impersonation of *Margaret*, notwithstanding it has moments of great charm, lacks, on the whole, distinction and is quite unworthy a place beside her *Beatrice* or her *Portia*. Although the figure of the innocent German maiden is always a sweet and gracious one, and although Miss Terry invests it with both these qualities, it somehow or other fails to move us as we know that such a figure ought. Where Miss Terry is most at fault is in those earlier scenes which demand the utmost limit of artlessness and unsophistication. Her girlish raptures over the jewels do not strike an altogether natural note, despite all her pretty attitudinizing.

Miss Terry is altogether better in the rather trying scenes before and within the church ; but taken as a whole her *Margaret* can only be accepted by those whose intense personal admiration for the artist blinds them to every defect. Too many critics, we may add, have been thus affected. Mr. Alexander's *Faust* we have always considered dry and hard. It has moments of force and dignity, but it lacks the elasticity and vigour of youth. Mrs. Chippendale portrays that excellent but coarse old woman, *Martha*, with a steady and clever hand, and the rest of the Lyceum company fill out the smaller parts with ability and discretion.

"Olivia," which was originally written by Mr. W. G. Wills for Miss Terry's especial benefit, was first produced in America ten years ago. The part of the *Vicar* has been played by Mr. William Warren, and Miss Annie Clarke and Miss Fanny Davenport have each been seen in the title-rôle. But it is fair to assume that the play is unfamiliar enough to theatre-goers to make a brief discussion of its qualities not altogether superfluous.

It must be remarked at the outset that those people who do not take the statement made on the programme in its most literal sense will suffer at first from a feeling of, perhaps not disappointment, but bewilderment. "Olivia" is not in any sense a dramatization of "The Vicar of Wakefield ;" it is, as the author has always been careful to insist, merely "founded on an episode" in Goldsmith's exquisite story. It would be in the highest degree unjust, therefore, to discuss it altogether from the point of view of its relation to that story. The manner of the narrative is essentially undramatic; and so, too, is much of the matter. To have followed with any attempt at precision the lines laid down there would have entailed the construction of an elaborate and complicated drama, which from the very nature of the limitations imposed by the stage could not have had the artistic force and coherence of " The Vicar of Wakefield." Had Mr. Wills kept such a purpose in his mind, he would speedily have found himself entangled in a maze of absurdities. Between the simplicity of Goldsmith and the intricacy of Dickens there is, of course, a wide and vital distinction; but something of the same embarrassment which has followed the adapters of the latter author would have pursued Mr. Wills had he endeavoured to keep to the beaten track marked out by them. But the story of *Olivia's* disgrace and restoration, reduced to its simplest terms, is a theme primarily dramatic in its force and intensity. More than this, it derives a human interest at once powerful and beautiful from the presence of the *Vicar*, himself one of the most charming creations in the whole range of literature, drawn with a largeness and comprehensiveness of outline which makes it possible to present him to the outward eye chiefly in connection with his daughter, without at the same time robbing him of any of the essential attributes of his personality. The artistic value of Mr. Wills's play, therefore, is very largely due to his careful observance of these limits. What he actually eliminates from the novel may be very briefly stated. Misfortune does not fall upon the family of the *Vicar* until after *Squire Thornhill* and *Burchell* have each become visitors at the vicarage. The affairs of the eldest son *George* are entirely dismissed, and *Miss Wilmot* and the *Squire's* intended marriage with her are alike passed over ; and such persons as the London women who talked of " pictures, taste, Shakspere, and the musical glasses," are also necessarily ignored. *Moses* is introduced, but we hear nothing of the green spectacles; while both *Olivia* and *Sophia* are given a touch of serious sweetness which the author of their being denied them. The necessity for dramatic compactness and directness has also led Mr. Wills to modify materially the later portions of the story. The masquerading *Burchell* asserts his ownership of the name and title of *Sir William Thornhill* at a period in the play where he can more effectually cow and confound his graceless nephew ; and even before this he has quietly relieved the *Vicar* from his financial troubles in such a way that he is spared the sad experience of imprisonment. The play opens in the vicarage garden, on the day of the good *Doctor's* silver wedding, which his parishioners gather to celebrate. *Thornhill* and *Burchell* both appear as guests and the object of the visit of each is made clear from the outset. The second act shows us the vicarage parlour, which becomes in time the scene of the *Squire's* efforts to induce *Olivia* to elope with him and of *Burchell's* ill-appreciated endeavours at once to do the family a benevolent turn and to save it from impending disgrace. It closes with a beautiful picture of the family gathered about the old spinet to sing the evening hymn, of which the harmony is only too rudely interrupted by the discovery of *Olivia's* flight. We are then taken to the Dragon Inn, where the unfortunate girl first learns the cruel deception which has been practised upon her and where she is finally found and taken home by her father. The play closes in the vicarage parlour again, where the tangled thread of dishonour is unwound by the discovery that the mock marriage was a real one, after all.

This brief sketch will make clear enough the manner in which Mr. Wills has made use of the too-abundant materials in Goldsmith's story. Sticklers for exact literary propriety who have more ingenuity than discrimination can no doubt point out flaws enough both in the scheme and in its execution. But we do not anticipate being disputed by any one competent to pass judgment in such matters when we assert that for the purposes of the stage it would be hard to make a better selection. Where Mr. Wills has borrowed Goldsmith's language he has done so with equal taste and reverence; where he has supplied a text of his own—as he is constantly compelled to do—the same admirable qualities of mind and temper have not been wanting. For our own part, we suspect that those who find their sensibilities outraged by what they would call tampering with a classic would confess, if the question were put squarely to them, that they are unwilling to admit the lawfulness of casting any product of the imagination in another than its original mould. It is well to respect the intention of an author, but it may be pointed out that literary worship not unfrequently reaches a pitch of jealous arrogance with which it is impossible to feel much sympathy. Shakspere adapted by Cibber or Garrick is an intellectual crime because the attempt is made to reshape in a worse fashion and for the same purpose work that is in itself imperishably great ; but an endeavour to bring to the actuality of the stage an episode or a character unconsciously endowed by its creator with dramatic worth and permanence should receive, it seems to us, the encouragement commensurate with its degree of success. And Mr. Wills, whose worth and capacity as a playwright have been strangely overlooked by most of his critics, has brought to his task in this instance those qualities of skill, discrimination and delicacy which demand the warmest approval.

The manner in which "Olivia" is presented by Mr. Irving and his intelligent and carefully-trained company cannot be too highly commended. The play does not offer those opportunities for scenic magnificence which have sometimes made the fortune of a pretty bare and poor performance. But the simple and idyllic beauty of the settings make an appeal to the eye which not even the least observant spectator can disregard and which confer upon every person of the least æsthetic sensibility a very high degree of enjoyment. No detail which will heighten the fidelity of the picture is omitted ; but at the same time the general effect is never lost in mere elaboration. The visit of the parishioners to the *Vicar* presents to the eye any number of interesting studies in country life in England in the eighteenth century ;

and the exterior of the house, the garden and the
landscape illumined by the setting sun in the distance
have a soft and genial charm such as painters upon
stage canvas seldom know how to reproduce. The
two interiors are equally refined in conception and
faithful in detail. The lattice with its diamond panes,
the old and quaint furnishings, elegant in their simplicity, the tall clock in the corner with its silver chime,
the shelf of books and the spinet—on each and all of
these the eye delights to linger. Nor is the room in
the inn, though necessarily less inviting than the
vicarage parlour which contains these treasures, less
harmonious in design, however much it may lack the
homeliness (using the word in its proper sense) of the
other. Of the picturesqueness and effectiveness of the
grouping something has already been said; but we
must not forget perhaps the most charm'ng picture of
all—that scene where *Olivia* takes her unconsciously
pathetic farewell of her mother by the fireplace, while
Sophia and the children gather opposite and the good
Vicar and *Mr. Burchell* play at chess in the capacious
window-seat in the background. Another touch
characteristic of Mr. Irving is the chiming of the bells
and the music of the organ to the sweet and familiar
hymn of Haydn's, " Sun of my Soul," at the very
moment when *Dr. Primrose*, at the end of the happy
evening of the silver wedding, gathers his family about
him to tell them of their misfortune. Such sights and
sounds as these linger long and graciously in the
memory of the spectator.

Of Mr. Irving's impersonation of *Dr. Primrose*
there is so much that might be said that one is fairly

at a loss where to begin and where to end. We fancy
that to the majority of those who have had the good
fortune to see it, it is a new and singular revelation
of his capacity as an artist of very high rank. We
do not mean by this that such impersonations as his
Shylock, his *Hamlet*, his *Mathias*, his *Louis XI.*, and
his *Mephistopheles* have not been in their differing
degrees and qualities sufficient witnesses of the
validity of his claim to the careful attention of students of the stage ; but what we wish to insist upon
is that all of these have a certain interdependence and
coherence—widely apart in motive and execution as
each is from the other—which bring to those who have
seen him only in them an impression of the limits
of his dramatic capacity which his *Dr. Primrose* at
once destroys. Even in the comedy of *Benedick* and
Malvolio—those two parts which we agree with an
eminent critic in thinking altogether inferior to his
general work—there is nothing that prepares one for
the ideal and idyllic quality which permeates his conception of the good old *Vicar*. Mr. Irving's general
method unfortunately inclines rather to the realistic ;
leaving the impersonation of *Dr. Primrose* out of
account, indeed, one would find a measure of justification in characterizing him as a realist without
qualification. But to appreciate this fine and exquisite
piece of art, nothing is more essential than that
previous impressions, however well grounded, should
be left out of the account. The simplicity, affection,
fervour and pervading piety of the *Vicar's* character
are presented by Mr. Irving with equal force and
delicacy, and with a freedom from mere dramatic cant

and affectation that is at once refreshing and touching.
Indeed, Mr. Irving has here purged his acting quite as
completely from mere mannerism as any artist of
intense individuality can well do ; and the only
reminiscence of that mannerism which can at all offend
even the most sensitive hearer is the occasional lapse
into that unpleasant quality of voice which is perhaps
his most serious (certainly his most obvious) defect.
The tenderness and simple beauty of his kindliness
towards his friends and neighbours and his affection
for his family are exquisitely portrayed. The depth
and sincerity of his love for his erring daughter, which
he thinks of as idolatry, and endeavours to stifle now
and then with ill success, are further touches which
partake of much that is true in nature and exquisite
in art. Nowhere, perhaps, is the essentially human
goodness of the old man made manifest with more
distinctness than in the scene where the first impulse
of the moment leads him to curse and vow vengeance
upon his daughter's betrayer and the second impulse
brings him to feel the truth of his wife's appeal that the
Bible is a fitter weapon for his hand than the pistol, or
again in the scene where his effort to play the preacher
to the erring and repentant one is mastered at a stroke
by the power of fatherly love. There are other passages as exquisite as these, upon which space forbids
us to linger, but none more vivid and immediately
impressive. How far Mr. Irving's impersonation as a
whole differs from that of Mr. Warren to which we
have already referred it is not necessary—it might at
this distance be impossible—to consider. Speaking
under the possibility of correction, we can only say

N

that Mr. Irving's conception of the *Vicar* seems to us less absolutely ideal than Mr. Warren's (though still, as we have pointed out, with an ideality by no means slight) and perhaps less bucolic, using the word in no invidious sense, than his. We need not add that these distinctions, slight as they are, do not greatly affect the value of the English actor's work, which, to sum up, is to be highly commended for its sincerity and beauty.

Charming as Miss Terry's impersonation of *Olivia* is in detached passages, it will not, as a whole, bear comparison with Mr. Irving's *Dr. Primrose.* In the earlier scenes Miss Terry plays with a good deal of gaiety and lightness of touch; but here again, as in her *Margaret,* there is a too pervading air of deliberation and self-consciousness. She portrays the sweet simplicity of an English girl a century ago far less effectively than does Miss Winifred Emery, whose *Sophia* in this same play is a charming picture of unaffected modesty and kindly cheerfulness. Her petulant disappointment at her lover's delay, well-expressed as it is, gives the spectator an impression of worldly experience quite foreign to the character of *Olivia,* although nothing could be better in its way than the reproachful manner with which she chides him when he comes at last. The struggle between her doubts and hopes in the scene where the *Squire* urges her to fly with him is also indicated with many exquisite touches; and in her farewell to the family, one member after another, there is a pathetic quality which moves the imagination, if it does not precisely reach the heart. In the trying

situation of the third act Miss Terry deserves a
much greater degree of commendation. Although
by all odds the most delightful thing in the whole
impersonation is *Olivia's* childish delight at the pro-
spect of seeing her home once more in the happy
Christmas season (leaving out of account the hop-
skip-and-a-jump passages which have no dramatic
meaning whatever and perhaps on that account
please audiences so greatly), the swiftly following
surprise, incredulity, horror, anger and defiance of
the powerful scene in which *Squire Thornhill* reveals
to her amazed and bewildered mind the fatal truth,
are touches which may be praised with comparatively
little critical deduction. But it should be pointed
out that in the very climax of *Olivia's* grief and
despair Miss Terry falls short of the highest artistic
force. In the utterance of the one expressive and
inclusive word, " Devil ! " she fails to reach the fervid
intensity which. as some of the readers of this account
may recall, characterized Miss Annie Clarke's impersonation ten years ago. And although, as we have
already said, Miss Terry's impersonation has here a
pathetic quality, it falls short of any tragic power.
We need hardly add that we do not agree with
those critics who have found this power in Miss
Terry's work. In our opinion that artist is at her
best when she has the opportunity simply to be
graceful, tender and womanly ; and it is in precisely
the passages in *Olivia* which give her this opportunity that she is altogether satisfying. Mr. Alexander
gives the graceless *Squire* just the right proportion
of audacity and cynical insolence, keeping within a

certain limit of manliness, which prepares one in a
degree for his sudden change of heart at the close.
The part is not only one of the most difficult which
Mr. Alexander has attempted here, but it is one of
the very best among all the impersonations of the
sort which we have ever witnessed. He keeps the
villainy of the *Squire* absolutely free from that melodramatic flavour which many actors (perhaps most
actors) would have given it, and makes it a clear,
consistent and altogether admirable presentation of
a well-defined type of character. His disclosure to
Olivia of the deception he has practised upon her is
both logical and forcible in its alternations of reluc-
tance and *insouciance*, and his manner to *Burchill*,
both before and after the revelation of the latter's
identity, is most appropriate. Of Miss Emery's exquisite impersonation of *Sophia* any elaborate analysis
will not be necessary. The part is too quiet and
too completely subordinated to that of *Olivia* to
give it the value in the eyes of an audience which
the rare discrimination and delicacy of Miss Emery's
manner of playing it really deserves ; yet, as has been
observed on a preceding page, it is hardly to be surpassed as a bit of faithful and artistic portraiture.
One or two more scenes as brightly and cleverly
done as the little discussion of household troubles
with *Mr. Burchill* over the tea-table could hardly
have left even the dullest spectator without a sense
of the genuine beauty of the impersonation. But
however the popular taste of the day may run to
violence rather than strength, the feeling of artistic
coherency and proportion shown by Miss Emery in

this instance deserves the warmest critical recognition. Mr. Wenman's *Burchill* has force, dignity and
manly eloquence, to whatever degree it may lack
the subtler touches and the more delicate shades of
dramatic art. He is at his very best and strongest
in the scene with the *Squire* in the third act. Mr.
Howe's study of the honest *Farmer Hamborough*,
blunt, rough and incapable of understanding the
Vicar but not of being touched by his goodness, has
all the singular care and finish of the old school of
acting of which we have to-day two few representatives. Mrs. Pauncefort deserves a word of moderate
praise as *Mrs. Primrose*.

Mr. Irving's impersonation of *Shylock* is too
familiar to need elaborate analysis at our hands.
But an increased acquaintance with it does not con-
vince us that his conception of the character is in any
way a just or accurate one. The most impressive
thing about *Shylock* is the fact that he is an incarnation of his nationality. The picture is not complete;
even Shakspere was not so entirely isolated from
mediæval prejudices as to do full justice to the Jewish
character, although the moral difference between "The
Merchant of Venice" and Marlowe's "Jew of Malta"
is very great. But that Shakspere intended to
emphasize the national rather than the personal
characteristics of *Shylock* there can be no manner of
doubt.

> I hate him, for he is a Christian;
> But more, for that in low simplicity
> He lends out money gratis and brings down
> The rate of usance here with us in Venice.

Both charges against the merchant are made with distinctness enough; but the first strikes, we think, the keynote of Shakspere's conception. And we cannot feel that Mr. Irving makes this point clear enough. As for the general aspects of his impersonation, it need only be said that while he is vivid, intense and malignant to a degree in portraying the baser attributes of *Shylock's* character, he fails, on the whole, to give the man that touch of dignity which raises him a little above the mean and malicious usurer. We feel this especially in the scene with *Tubal;* elsewhere through the early portions of the play the manifestations of cunning, hatred, rage and revenge are distinct and powerful enough. In the fourth act Mr. Irving reaches a higher point of exact and impressive delineation of character. So thoroughly consistent and so finely human does he make *Shylock* here that the spectator is compelled to sympathize, against his will, with the man's utter defeat and discomfiture. Mr. Irving's face and attitude as he leaves the presence of the court, cowed but not subdued, must fill a memorable place in the imagination of every beholder.

In *Portia* Miss Terry gives us a charming picture of generous womanhood that is also not easily obliterated from one's recollections. Her mingled anxiety and indifference over the results of the choice among the caskets; her maidenly frankness in her confession of love to *Bassanio* and her touching self-abnegation when she finds that he has chosen aright; her womanly confidences with *Nerissa;* her raillery of her husband when he returns without the ring—all these are touches the beauty and value of which it would be impossible to praise too highly. And in the trial scene the exquisite propriety with which she delivers the speech—

> The quality of mercy is not strained,

is something which no one who has heard it would willingly forget. Unless *Beatrice* be excepted, we know of no other impersonation of Miss Terry's which is on the whole so delightful as this. Her *Portia* shows at once the range and the limitations of her genius, and it leaves a pleasanter impression than such unsatisfactory performances as her *Margaret* and her *Olivia*. Mr. Alexander's *Bassanio* is manly and fervid, Miss Emery's *Jessica* shows how beautifully an accomplished artist can play a comparatively insignificant part and Mr. Wenman's *Antonio* has gratifying strength and solidity. Of the charming pictures or Venetian life presented in the setting of the play we need say nothing at this late day.

In the opinion of more than one competent critic Mr. Irving's impersonation of *Mathias* in "The Bells" is the most impressive and powerful thing he does. Impressive and powerful it certainly is; but, as we have already said, it is always difficult and usually impossible, to say of any single work from the hand of a great artist that it is absolutely his best. And where such a singularly diverse performance in dramatic art as Mr. Irving has already accomplished is to be considered, hasty generalization is especially deplorable. Without splitting of hairs as to place or

degree, however, it is enough to say of his *Mathias*
that it is, within certain narrow limits, an impersonation at once so vivid and so forcible that it seizes upon
the imagination of the spectator with an unrelenting
and almost painful intensity, and lingers in the memory
with inlelible distinctness. To our own mind, there
are other impersonations of Mr. Irving's which better
show the true breadth and range of his talent than
his *Mathias;* but in no one of them is a certain phase
of that talent—by no means the least admirable
phase—more clearly indicated. *Mathias* is a character
of melodrama, if you choose; certainly he is no such
illimitable and enduring type as (let us say) *Macbeth*.
It might be argued that a man capable of so cold-
blooded a crime would never be perpetually harassed
by the pangs of remorse, however open he might be
to merely physical terrors. Mr. Irving shows a just
appreciation of this difficulty by emphasizing the
latter aspect of the case. He makes it clear that
what most haunts the man is the fear of detection,
and that the purely nervous dread of the bells which
ring now and then in his ears with awful meaning
proceeds from and emphasizes this fact. Like *Macbeth*, however, *Mathias* is pursued by the phantoms
which a diseased imagination perpetually conjures up.
The loneliness and the darkness bring horrible visions.
When the house is quiet he lives the deed all over
again, and fancies the apparition is before his eyes as
it is before those of the audience. When, for fear of
blabbing the secret in his sleep, he locks himself into
a lonely chamber, another horrible phantasmagoria
passes before his eyes - an image of his trial and con-

demnation by ghostly judges. Here, we see, is still
the same truth enforced; it is dread, and not remorse,
that harasses him. Mr. Irving portrays the man's
abandonment and despair vividly and impressively.
So finely and so truly is it done that one half expects
to see the actor's visible and tangible self break forth
from behind the curtains of his bed in waking terror
at the ghastly dream which is being brought before
the eyes of the audience by himself. One cannot
even write of that awful scene without a tremor, as
if it were once more visible to the outward sense.
And the face of *Mathias* as he staggers forth after the
phantoms of which his own image was the centre have
vanished, in its haggard and insane frenzy, is itself
an apparition which nothing can obliterate from the
imagination of the beholder.

Of the lighter and more humane touches in Mr.
Irving's impersonation a great deal might be said with
satisfaction, and possibly to advantage. But "The
Bells" is not unfamiliar to theatre-goers, and it will
not be necessary to enlarge upon these points now.
Throughout the whole of the second act the essentially
base nature of the man is skilfully indicated, the
mixture of greed and cunning in the counting out of
the daughter's dowry, the ghastly merriment at the
young officer's suggestion that the body of the Jew
might have been destroyed in one of the lime-kilns
and the politic eagerness to have the marriage contract signed being among the more significant features
of the delineation. The one redeeming trait of this
ignoble nature, *Mathias's* love for his daughter, is also
beautifully developed by Mr. Irving. In the character

of this daughter, Miss Winifred Emery is thoroughly charming. It is not, apart from its environment, an especially significant part, and it is negatively rather than positively developed by the dramatist. But Miss Emery's artistic method is so natural and genuine, her taste is so fine and discriminating and (what is of less importance, perhaps) her personal charm is so constant and pervasive, that she lifts it at once to a very high level and endows it with a dramatic quality that at once appeals to the imagination of the spectator. The quietly tender and exquisitely human passages with father and lover could hardly, it seems to us, be better portrayed. Mr. Alexander, though too laboured and emotionally impassive, appears to very good advantage as the young officer, and Mrs. Pauncefort also deserves a word of moderate commendation.

"Jingle," a lively little farce taken, as its name indicates, from the "Pickwick Papers," is played as an after-piece to the more serious play. Even so slight a sketch as this is put upon the stage with as much care as an important piece would be, and all the characters, particularly *Mr. Pickwick* himself, look as if they had stepped bodily from Cruikshank's pictures. Mr. Irving's *Jingle* is thoroughly clever, bright, vivacious, and amusing, and his air of volatile impudence is well sustained throughout. Mr Howe's *Pickwick* and Mr. Harbury's *Tupman* deserve especial mention among the rest of the many small parts introduced.

Both the play of "The Lyons Mail" and Mr.

Irving's dual impersonation of *Lesurques* and *Dubosc* are more or less familiar to all play-goers, and it will therefore not be necessary to discuss either at this late day with any effort at precision or fulness. The drama has the picturesqueness and vigour which may perhaps be accepted as the prime characteristics of the author's work. While Charles Reade was always primarily a novelist, his genius had a certain vivid and pithy quality which fitted him by no means ill for the task of the dramatist. If one recalls the scenes from his stories which linger longest in the imagination, one will find, in nine cases out of ten, that they are precisely those episodes which lend themselves most readily to dramatic treatment. The value of Reade's work was under-estimated during his life, and in his death he has not been honoured to the degree which his singular and varied powers properly demand. Such a play as " The Lyons Mail " has its faults, no doubt ; but the worst that can be said of it, after all, is that in more than one place it inclines to the melodramatic rather than the absolutely artistic. Impressive as the main incident and most of the subsidiary episodes are, the play as a whole falls short of absolute greatness from the occasional coarseness and heaviness of touch which differentiates melodrama from drama pure and simple. Yet it offers an agreeable contrast to the great bulk of plays—outside of the recognized stage classics—in having a serious interest, consistently and firmly developed. In the second act, in particular, the play of human emotion follows obviously from the surroundings, and nothing is brought into exaggerated prominence to enhance a situation or prepare a climax. The characters of *Dubosc* and *Lesurques* are well drawn, each in its way; and, although the former is no doubt the more striking, it cannot be said that it keeps, on the whole, closer to nature. And whatever flaws may be discovered here and there in the texture of the piece, one is too grateful for the literary touch which betrays the hand of genius not to be indulgent on this point.

Nothing that Mr. Irving attempts presents so many substantial difficulties, in our opinion, as his dual impersonation in this play. And while his work here does not stand the test of comparison with Mdme. Janauschek's remarkable dual impersonation in "Bleak House," it is also remarkable in its way. But without entering into comparisons, which, as we have more than once asserted in these pages, are usually profitless and misleading, it is enough to say that such a performance as this which we are considering might stand alone in evidence of Mr. Irving's real ability as an artist. What strikes a thoughtful observer first of all, perhaps, is the ability to make the inward man visible in the outward expression. No other change is necessary to transform *Lesurques* and *Dubosc* beyond the deep significance expressed in the countenance of each. So vivid and distinct is the difference between the honest man and the thief that no one could possibly mistake one for the other if the two could be placed side by side. The confusion of identity is made natural and inevitable in the case of the companions of each, especially at the first hasty glance; at the same time the spectator is so impressed from the very outset with the wide moral gulf between the two, that it hardly needs the slight variety of costume which Mr. Irving adopts to make one inevitably and immutably divisible from the other. Without dwelling upon this point (and only pausing to remark upon the clever device in the last act by which *Lesurques* appears at the door as *Dubosc* rushes forth from his hiding-place and is caught and pinioned by the angry mob), some of the striking characteristics of both impersonations may be briefly recalled to the reader. *Lesurques* is beau· tifully consistent throughout, and the clear honesty and nobility of the man are drawn with a delicate and thoroughly artistic touch. But above even these stand his sensitive honour and his parental tenderness. When the base accusation is first brought against him, he smiles at the error; he feels that his reputation is too securely grounded to be tarnished by the breath of scandal. But as the horrible suspicion is reflected with more and more certainty in the faces of those around him, his whole soul revolts in a passionate appeal for incredulity. And through all the trying moment his love for his innocent daughter remains to comfort and strengthen him. In the scene in the prison courtyard this quality of the man's nature finds its most perfect development, just as in the painful interview with his father his innate nobility finds its highest expression in his refusal to end his own life ignominiously. The most marked feature of *Dubosc's* character, on the other hand, is his utter selfishness and ignoble animalism. To the appeals of the woman he has ruined he pays absolutely no attention. He can threaten and abuse her, and even strike her to the ground ; and he can also reach the shameless point of declaring that she is the only woman he ever loved. His natural state is one of drunken ferocity ; and he is so far from being a clever villain that he recklessly brings about his own ruin in the end. Mr. Irving's acting in the last scene of this brutal assassin's existence is very natural in its manifestation of dogged sensuality and brute force.

The Lyceum company, on the whole, do excellent work in the less conspicuous parts. Miss Winifred Emery plays *Julie Lesurques* with genuine pathos and artistic force and imparts besides a rare personal charm to every scene in which she appears. Her simple and gracious kindliness to *Jeannette*, her frank affection for her lover, her devotion to her father, the sincerity and self-abnegation with which she clings to him in the darkest moments of his distress—these are one and all exquisite touches which deserve the heartiest praise. Her complete abandonment of grief as the hour for what each supposes to be the final parting approaches and the desperate tenacity with which she refuses to leave his side (beautifully expressed by the gesture repulsing even her betrothed husband) are portrayed with a depth and fervour in every way admirable and satisfying. Mr. Alexander gives the rascally *Courriol* too decided a touch of opera bouffe—the word is a harsh one, but we can think of no other which expresses our meaning—though he redeems himself by a single touch of nature at the end. Mr. Wenman's *Choppard* is better in its humour than in anything else, and Mr. Mead's *Jerome Lesurques* excels in quiet dignity and force. Miss Dietz is not to be credited with making much out of the part of *Jeannette*. As is the case in everything that Mr. Irving produces, the scenery and costumes are in the best of taste. There is just a little too much music from the orchestra now and then, and Mr. Irving's more explosive utterances are too often accentuated by a sob from the violins.

The chief personage in the play of "Louis XI." in the hands of Mr. Irving, takes to himself a personality full of strange attraction; he repels even the playgoer who has fed upon horrors and yet he would hold a wedding-guest with his glittering eye. Mr. Irving's *Louis* is not familiar here in the sense that Mr. Booth's impersonations, or even the better known among Signor Salvini's, are familiar; but to have seen it once seems to give the spectator an intimate acquaintance with it. When the king says: "I was a dauphin once;" or, after the death of his too-powerful vassal, *Charles of Burgundy*, "The court shall wear full mourning for a week;" or, when begging the holy *François de Paules* by some miraculous means to prolong his life, and, finding he has only religious counsel to bestow, he cries, "I have heard enough of that"—these are moments and phrases not to be forgotten, but quite impossible to describe. When *Louis* crouches before the fire to warm his shivering body, chilled already with the approach of death, and promises the Virgin chapels and rich gifts if she will forgive his sins, and more particularly one little sin he means to commit that night, a distinctly higher point of picturesque impression is reached; and the highest attainment in this kind which the impersonation offers has passed already into the annals of the stage. We mean, of course, the episode which finds *Louis* planning the death of *Nemours* and giving his secret instructions to *Tristan*, the bloody provost. The Angelus sounds, and the king—with the murder still in his heart which has just been upon his lips—takes off his cap, mumbles a few prayers to the images of saints that surround it and then returns to his vindictive work. The action, the look of blind superstition, the significance of the whole episode, make a lecture on the Dark Ages and some of the darker aspects of human nature for which one might look vainly in the pages of many a learned volume. In the opening scenes, Mr. Irving seemed to us to over-accentuate some points, but in the impersonation as a whole details were subdued to the main effect with most careful art. Of the supporting players it may be said that golden mediocrity was the rule—a rule to which Miss Winifred Emery, whose impersonation of *Marie* had the singular charm inseparable from all this delightful artist's work, and Mr. Alexander deserve to be excepted.

EDITOR.

SOME SHAKSPERIAN REVIVALS.

[MADAME MODJESKA.]

BEYOND the production of two Shaksperian plays seldom seen upon the stage, an account of which is given below, Mdme. Modjeska's season presents no incidents of prime importance. Her tour was an extended one and her engagements in New York and Boston were only for a single fortnight. In the last-named city she met with signal success and drew crowded houses. Madame Modjeska's company proved to be, on the whole, a good one. All the leading members of it have at one time and another done excellent work. Mr. Eben Plympton has manifested great intelligence and breadth, considerable force and feeling (if now and then too loudly expressed) and much artistic sincerity of expression. If his *Angelo* and his *Armand* have not been altogether commendable, on the other hand his *Benedick* and his *Don Cæsar* have deserved the warmest admiration. Of Miss Mary Shaw it need only be said now and here that she is an artist of rare insight and intellectual discrimination, that her cultivated elocutionary method is a constant delight to the ear and that whatever part she undertakes she endows with life and individuality. Mr. Vandenhoff, despite a certain hardness of manner, should be included among the valuable members of

O

the company, as also Mr. Owen—one of the most delightful interpreters of Shaksperian humour whom we have seen in many a day—and young Mr. Taber, an actor of intelligence and promise. Miss Clara Ellison, too, has done some small parts—notably *Floretta* in "Dona Diana"—delightfully well. Following are brief criticisms of the Shaksperian revivals which, as we have said, chiefly characterized Madame Modjeska's season.

If Mdme. Modjeska had done nothing else than rescue "Measure for Measure" from its long disuse as an acting play she would have earned the cordial approval of every real believer in the worth and dignity of the stage. A word upon the play— which, if we are not mistaken, has not been seen upon the stage here, with the exception of its presentation by Miss Adelaide Neilson eight years ago, for half a century or more—will not be out of place, in spite of its ready accessibility to readers of Shakspere.

Obvious as the debt to the Italian Cinthio is, it is the English Shakspere who gives the story its permanent ethical value. Shakspere, indeed, owed nothing to Cinthio beyond a bare outline of the plot, and he materially modified even this in order to preserve unimpaired the sweet and gracious purity of *Isabella*. The introduction of *Mariana* for this purpose has been condemned by critics who have been unable to understand the delicacy of dramatic feeling which made such an innovation in Cinthio's story a necessity with Shakspere; but no person

competent of understanding rightly the play will take
issue, we fancy, with his judgment in this respect.
"Measure for Measure," indeed, moves so nearly in
tragic lines that only by such a device as this can
Isabella take her place with *Portia* and *Imogen* rather
than with *Volumnia* and *Constance*.   This tragic
underlying *motif* struck Coleridge so forcibly that
he called the play the "least agreeable" of Shakspere's dramas ; but this was a rather superficial
piece of criticism.   "Measure for Measure" is surely
not disagreeable, if we use the word in the only sense
in which it properly can be used in such a connection ;
that it should have been so characterized by Coleridge may be explained perhaps by what Verplanck
calls "the impressive power with which it enforces
revolting and humbling truths."   But as the same
critic points out, "though the subject and the
thoughts be in themselves repulsive, yet when, as
here, we feel that the author is breathing through
them the strong emotions of his own soul, the attention is fixed and the sympathy enchained."   That
these were the strong emotions of Shakspere's own
soul the fact that "Measure for Measure" is nearly
identical in time with "Hamlet" (the date is pretty
certainly 1603) is strong evidence.   There are not a
few parallelisms between the two plays, a fact which
it might be interesting, had we the time and space,
to point out.   It is enough to observe here the
divergence of purpose which led the dramatist
to make one a comedy and the other a tragedy.
That the story of *Isabella* might easily have been
used for tragic purposes the existence of Whetstone's

" Promos and Cassandra " readily suggests. Various critics have argued with some force that Shakspere was indebted quite as much to Whetstone as to Cinthio ; and Mr. Collier quotes a passage in " Promos and Cassandra : "

> Who others doth deceyve
> Deserves himself like measure to receyve,

as possibly suggesting the title, " Measure for Measure." But against this we may properly set the fact that " Promos and Cassandra," by Whetstone's own confession in a translation of Cinthio's novel, was never performed ; and it is at least open to question if Shakspere would have taken the pains to consult the printed copy, published in 1578, a quarter of a century before his own drama was written. The fact that Shakspere has in no case followed Whetstone in naming his *dramatis personæ*, though by no means conclusive proof upon this point, may at least be allowed to have some weight.

Of the many individual passages of great beauty in Shakspere's play it is not necessary here to speak. In perfection of poetic art and in sanity of ethical touch the verse is to be compared with that of " Hamlet," with which in point of time it is so closely linked. The air of the drama has been called stifling, and so in a degree it is ; but through all the beautiful and pure figure of *Isabella* sheds a light and fragrance which linger long in the memory. No other of Shakspere's women, unless it be *Portia*, betrays a more exquisite moral poise. There are other lines of coincidence with *Portia*, too, despite Mrs. Jameson's ingenious differentiation of the two women. Apart

from all comparisons, however, there is enough and
to spare of individual charm in *Isabella* to command
the highest admiration. Perhaps the most significant
single point in her character is the strong quality of
passionate enthusiasm which flashes out at crucial
moments above the calm dignity of her exterior. If
we admit this, the test of the ability of the artist to
give an adequate representation of the whole character
should be applied precisely here. So far as Mdme.
Modjeska is concerned, this test is eminently successful. In the scenes with *Angelo* and with her
brother her bitter outbursts of womanly indignation
make an admirable contrast with the sweet and saintly
stateliness of her customary bearing. Her eloquence
has all *Portia's* logic, enforced with a strong personal
sense of wrong and injustice. Mdme. Modjeska's
delivery of such speeches as

> O it is excellent
> To have a giant's strength, but it is tyrannous
> To use it like a giant,

or, again, her impressive appeal—

> Go to your bosom ;
> Knock there, and ask your heart what it doth know
> That's like my brother's fault ;

or, finally, when the real meaning of *Angelo's* words
burst upon her mind and she turns to him with
wrath and shame in every feature—

> Ha ! little honour to be much believed,
> And most pernicious purpose ! Seeming, seeming ;
> I will proclaim thee, Angelo ; look for 't !
> Sign me a present pardon for my brother
> Or with an outstretch'd throat I'll tell the world
> Aloud what man thou art—

these burn themselves indelibly into the imagination of the listener. We cannot recall a time when Mdme. Modjeska has ever evinced a greater degree of dramatic force than here, with the possible exception of the scene with *Claudio* which follows. Here her swift and severe denunciation of him, "O you beast! O faithless coward!" is in every way finely and adequately expressive of the sudden loathing and contempt with which his base supplication has filled her. Nothing in the whole impersonation deserves higher praise than these passages to which we have referred, though everywhere the refined and thoroughly artistic method of the impersonator is agreeably felt. Among the most exquisite of the lighter touches is the manner of *Isabella's* plea to the *Duke* for *Angelo's* life. To sum up, then, Mdme. Modjeska's characterization has all those qualities of delicacy, grace and absolute naturalness and sincerity which we have long since learned to expect from her ; and it has besides a brilliancy and a force to which she has not often been equal. It must be added that it partakes to some extent of the faults discoverable in all her work—too great deliberation at some moments and a tendency towards sentimentalism at others.

The general arrangement of "Measure for Measure" for stage purposes and the acting done by the company are both commendable, though upon these points we must be brief. An outline of the scheme of the play as presented will best suffice for comment upon the first point. Those scenes offensive to modern taste are judiciously excised, though not too much emasculated ; and one or two of the less important of them are omitted altogether. We must protest, however, against the substitution of less direct and not more modest phrases for such expressions as "He hath got his friend with child," as well as the absurd change of "body" to "person" and the use of the expression, "naughty house." There were other misplacings of words and phrases which were quite unnecessary ; but some of these may have been the fault of the speakers. For the rest, Mdme. Modjeska's version runs about as follows : Act i. is given with substantial accuracy, a part of scene 2 being omitted ; act ii. includes i., 4, and ii., 1 and 2, with a single transposition act iii. includes ii., 4 ; act iv. begins with iii., 1, and runs on through the first three scenes of iv., with a few omissions ; and act v. is the fifth act of the original substantially as written. Except in the directions we have indicated, the text has been, on the whole, judiciously treated. The supporting company do fairly good work, Miss Shaw's *Mariana* and Mr. Vandenhoff's *Duke* deserving first mention, although, perhaps, the last-named places too much stress upon *Lucio's* characterization of the man as "the fantastic duke of dark corners." Mr. Plympton is at times impressive as *Angelo;* but his conception of the part ill accords with Shakspere's own, and no one would take him even at the outset to be one "whose blood is very snow-broth." Mr. Taber is excellent as *Claudio,* and Mr. Owen's *Pompey* is a delicious bit of humour.

"Cymbeline" is a more familiar play to theatre-goers than "Measure for Measure," but even it has been seen upon the stage much less often than one could wish. Although by general consent one of Shakspere's latest plays—the date having now been fixed with some certainty at 1610-11—it has never seemed to us equal to the other productions of this closing period of his career of authorship. In the interest of its story, in the conduct of incident, in grasp of character and in nobility of poetic diction it is inferior, not only to the recognized masterpieces of Shakspere's great third period of intellectual activity, but even to its immediate neighbours in point of time. The story is derived from at least two separate sources, Holinshed's Chronicle and a story in " Boccaccio ; " while the incidents relating to the two princes and their life in the mountains of Wales appear to have been a piece of pure invention. Perhaps it is for this reason that the piece strikes one as loosely constructed and as having no such strong dramatic coherence as even Shakspere's other romantic dramas, such as " The Tempest " and " The Winter's Tale ; " nor does it ever reach so high a level of pure poetry as either of these two. So far as it has to do with *Imogen*, however, it has an indubitable charm. We cannot agree with Professor Dowden that *Imogen* is " one of the loveliest of Shakspere's creations of female character," though she is certainly a woman who demands, like *Miranda*, the " top of admiration." But she has never been to us—though the fault may be in ourselves—quite so clear and vivid a character as *Portia*, or *Isabella*, or *Desdemona* or *Hermione*. Between *Imogen* and *Hermione* there is a strong connecting link, in so far that both are suspected unjustly by their husbands, one for apparent cause, the other for none at all. Notwithstanding the fact, however, that *Imogen* is an elaborate study and *Hermione* little more than a sketch, it is *Hermione* who seems to us to be the more finely and distinctly drawn. But apart from all this there is enough in the character of *Imogen* to make the impersonation one worthy of an artist; and there is certainly enough in the play to make its revival a matter for gratitude. To attempt to point out the defects of either is after all a good deal like searching for spots in the sun. Yet before we leave the subject it is worth while to insist upon what more than one critic has declared to be the weak point in " Cymbeline." The wager between *Posthumus* and *Iachimo* is a trick quite unworthy of the former; and however much one may detest the villainy which comes of it, one finds it difficult to acquit a husband who is willing to make a stake of his wife's honour from what is at least perilously near unmanly bravado.

Again, as in " Measure for Measure," Mdme. Modjeska has arranged the play very judiciously for the stage. There are few transpositions of any account, and few omissions of importance beyond the second scene of the fifth act, which is such a palpable absurdity that there is good ground for regarding it as a mere interpolation. Her impersonation of *Imogen* deserves on the whole, a considerable degree of praise. It has not quite the force and dignity of her *Isabella*, nor has it the exquisite charm of her *Viola*. The evil days and evil tongues upon which *Imogen's* life has fallen offer a temptation to an over-elaboration of grief and melancholy which Mdme. Modjeska·does not always resist. But after this deduction has been made there

remains a great deal which must be commended with
little qualification.   Mdme. Modjeska is always successful in portraying *Imogen's* wifely tenderness and
her well-nigh sublime quality of devotion to the absent
Leonatus, even in the face of the most cruel persecu-
tions.   Her exclamations at his departure—

> There cannot be a pinch in death
> More sharp than this is—

sets the very key-note of the impersonation.   After
this it is a time of enforced widowhood with her,
bitter as death itself.   Another note which may fairly
be called impressive is the quiet dignity with which
she rebuffs every attempt to make her forget her
husband.   As she tells her father—

> Sir,
> It is your fault that I have loved Posthumus ;
> You bred him as my playfellow ; he is
> A man worth any woman.

Equally admirable, though in a less restrained and
perhaps not more forcible manner, is her indignant
answer to the base proposals of *Iachimo* and her
sarcastic retort, "You make amends."   And further
on, her horror-stricken incredulity and grief at the
shameful charge preferred against her by her husband
are finely true to nature.   In the phrase of *Pisanio*,
"the paper hath cut her throat already ;" no other
misery is possible to a proud and faithful woman
thus outraged in all her deepest sensibilities.   Nor
must we forget to speak of the most charming of all
the lighter touches of Mdme. Modjeska's impersonation—her pretty bravado and her involuntary con-

fession of her woman's fears when, in the garb of a boy, she stands in fearful expectation before the cave of *Belarius*.

The work done by the company is in the main excellent. Mr. Plympton's *Leonatus* is one of the least agreeable of all his efforts, and it is too boisterous and flamboyant in almost every respect, though it is always intelligent and occasionally inspiring. But it is not worth a place beside such an admirable characterization as his *Don Cæsar* in " Dona Diana," or as his *Orlando*, to which reference is made below. Mr. Vandenhoff's *Iachimo* is well-defined and interesting ; but it lacks subtlety and plasticity. Mr. Taber plays *Pisanio* with evident care and intelligence, and Mr. Owen does good work in the part of *Cloten*. No one else deserves individual mention, unless it be Miss Sara Blanche Gray, and that only for her absolute inefficiency.

With " Much Ado about Nothing " it is certainly safe to assume a fair amount of familiarity. The play is not performed so often as one might wish ; but it was an important part of Mr. Irving's repertory during his first two seasons in this country and it was given with much success last winter by Miss Fanny Davenport. Possibly we do a very respectable part of the community an injustice ; but we confess to the feeling that any one of Shakspere's plays which is not often put upon the stage is practically neglected by all but the very few earnest students of the dramatist. As " Much Ado about Nothing " does not come within this category, there is no need to enter into any very elaborate discussion either of its place among the productions of its author or its qualities as a piece of dramatic art. It is worth while to remember that it falls in respect to its composition into what Mr. Furnival calls Shakspere's "bright, sweet time," probably coming between the "Merry Wives of Windsor" and "As You Like It." There are passages in it which recall the open and honest mirth of the early comedies, as well as passages which presage the working out of the more serious problems of life in "Measure for Measure," and "Julius Cæsar." It reveals its kinship with others of the later comedy group, by repeating, as Professor Dowden points out, "the incident of a trick or fraud practised upon one who is a self-lover." Thus *Benedick* or *Beatrice* have something in common, not only with *Orlando*, who is befooled by *Rosalind*, but even with *Falstaff*, *Malvolio* and *Parolles*, though in different degrees and with a different purpose. There is another stray connecting link between "Much Ado about Nothing" and "The Taming of the Shrew" to which, so far as we are aware, no one has yet called attention. *Beatrice* is a sweetened and softened *Katherine*—as independent and audacious, but more refined and womanly ; in other words, she is an intellectual shrew and she meets her match in one who uses her own weapons from the armoury of wit to take her fancy captive. But with all her merry captiousness she is so entirely human that she is by no means the least lovable of Shakspere's women ; and it is a serious mistake, in our opinion, to suppose that she needs sentimentalizing to make her acceptable to a nineteenth-century audience.

This is a mistake, unfortunately, which Mdme. Modjeska makes. With the exception of a single passage, where she hits more precisely the true Shaksperian note than most other actresses who have played the part have done, her *Beatrice* is on the whole rather a tender and tearful creature. That she can be exquisitely tender we know from her conduct to the betrayed and abandoned *Hero ;* but Mdme. Modjeska emphasizes this side of her nature too prematurely, so that the scene in the church strikes us less feelingly than it ought. The earlier speeches of *Beatrice* are continually thrust and parry, and here Mdme. Modjeska is wanting in brilliancy and in vigour. In several instances, too, she fails to give the full intellectual force of the passage. Occasionally in the rapid interchange of satire her difficulties with English speech make her well-nigh unintelligible. Yet it would be doing her an injustice not to recognize the aptness and force of her impersonation in many instances, particularly in the first scene of the second act. As we have already indicated, however, the very best portion of her work falls in the fourth act, in the scene with *Benedick*, which is inexcusably transferred from the church to some unnamed apartment, presumably in *Leonato's*, house. In one sense this scene offers the crucial test. It is here that Miss Terry failed to recognize the full meaning of *Beatrice's* attitude toward the man who has slandered her cousin ; but Mdme. Modjeska's quick and passionate demand, " Kill *Claudio !* " left nothing to be desired. And from that point onward her rage against *Claudio* was strongly and truly sustained. Here at last was a

Beatrice with a beating human heart! Miss Terry's *Beatrice* merely fell into a pretty pet; Mdme. Modjeska's rose to a height of genuine passion. There can be no doubt which of the two is Shakspere's. Had the rest of the impersonation maintained this high reach of artistic force and insight, it would have been almost an ideal one. But in the quieter scenes Mdme. Modjeska's desire to broaden and humanize *Beatrice* led her, as we have said, to the point of overflowing and excessive emotion.

With the exception of Miss Mary Shaw, whose *Hero* is a strong and well-developed impersonation, of which the art is well-nigh flawless; of Mr. Plympton, whose *Benedick* has a boisterous sort of humour and of dramatic reality; of Mr. Owen, whose *Dogberry* has the real Shaksperian flavour; of Mr. Vandenhoff, whose *Don Pedro*, though stiff and mannered, is effective in its sincerity; of Miss Clara Ellison, who plays the small part of *Margaret* with a light and facile touch; and of Mr. Taber, whose one brief scene as *Antonio* is well done, nothing need be said of the rest of the performance.

The other plays in which Madame Modjeska appeared during the season furnish her with parts too familiar to theatre-goers to need discussion here. Her impersonation of *Camille* deserves very little praise. It leaves no doubt in the mind that such a *Camille* as hers could not possibly be a just example of her class. The text is indeed always suggesting *Camille's* life and the place she holds in the world, but Mdme. Modjeska is ever gentle, sweet and pure, quite as much at the beginning as after suffering and grief have made pure the heart of the woman she presents. The impersonation is all in a lighter key than that of Sarah Bernhardt and the unequal but deeply moving performance in which Miss Morris has often been seen. Mdme. Modjeska's *Camille* is beautiful, often touching, but seldom the source of deep emotion ; and the tragic note which is frequently sounded by the author seems not to be within this lady's scope and ability. Mdme. Modjeska's *Viola*, on the other hand, is a most charming impersonation, and oné that even the most critical spectator cannot see too often. Some of the other parts are also notably well done, Mr. Owen's *Sir Toby*, Miss Shaw's *Olivia* (though we miss her in the part of *Maria*) and Mr. Taber's *Orsino* deserving especial mention. In *Mary Stuart*, Mdme. Modjeska is less happy in her characterization, in our opinion, and seldom gets below the surface of the part. Compared with that great representative of the Scottish Queen, Mdme. Janauschek, she is quite unsatisfactory. Miss Shaw does some brilliant work as *Queen Elizabeth*, even if at one or two moments, in the quarrel between the rivals, for instance, she fails to satisfy expectation. Mdme. Modjeska's charming impersonation of *Dona Diana* is familiar, and needs no fresh commendation now. Mr. Plympton plays *Don Cæsar* with much force and intelligence, as well as with more delicacy of feeling than usual. Mr. Owen does some work that is admirable in its humour, and Mr. Taber's *Don Louis* and Miss Clara Ellison's *Floretta* also deserve a word of praise.   EDITOR.

MR. BOUCICAULT AND IRISH DRAMA.

AT a superficial glance, Mr. Boucicault's play of
"Phryne," which was given—with marked success—
for the first time in our eastern towns, at the Hollis
Street Theatre, Boston, on the evening of October
17th, 1887, has about it a general atmosphere of
fastness, as "The Jilt" had a general atmosphere of
horsiness ; but on better acquaintance most of the
lions prove themselves sucking doves, and a play
which begins by suggesting Dumas *fils* ends in a
manner wholly worthy of the British matron. The
title of the piece is alarming, but the questionable
Greek lady whose name and fame have come down
to us among the other scandals of antiquity has
neither part nor lot in the character of *Phryne Carrington*, the beautiful young wife of a successful barrister and member of Parliament. Finding herself
left to dine alone on the first anniversary of their
marriage, as indeed has happened on many lesser
occasions, young *Mrs. Carrington* listens to the
promptings of *Mrs. Downey*, " a woman about town,"
and invites to celebrate the lonely anniversary the
members of a fastish club—called the Monte Carlo
—of which *Mrs. Downey* has had her made member.
Phryne's husband comes home in the midst of their very
innocent revels and makes a scene ; *Phryne*, showing
the spirit which is usually called " proper," proposes to

the club to finish the evening at their rooms ; and there
at one o'clock in the morning, she finds herself in a
repentant quandary, as *Carrington* has forbidden her
to enter his house again. *Mrs. Downey*, who is really
a kind-hearted, good sort of person, undertakes to
send *Phryne* in her carriage to a river-side cottage that
she possesses ; but *Vereker*, a wicked man·about town
and once a lover of *Phryne*, contrives to defeat *Mrs.
Downey* and send the unhappy young wife to his
own cottage at Wimbledon, where her husband finds
her next morning in *Vereker's* presence. There is no
way of proving her innocence to *Carrington ;* but two
years afterward—when in quite another neighbourhood *Phryne* is living as a nursery-governess in a comfortable house of her own—everything works itself
out for good in an agreeable fashion that the play-
goer shall be left to see for himself; and the
principal people of the play, good, bad and indifferent,
find themselves meeting under one roof according to
the pleasant custom so well known on the stage.
" Phryne " contains nothing that can strike the beholder as original, but—like most of Mr. Boucicault's
work—it is shrewdly devised and cleverly executed.
The characters are lightly drawn, but in most of them
shines the jewel of consistency ; and if one accepts the
situation at the beginning and continues to remember until the end that two or three of these characters
are supposed to be unusually good people and one
—at least—uncommonly bad, then conclusion follows premise with as much theatrical logic as one is
perhaps entitled to expect from " a domestic comedy-
drama in four acts." The dialogue is smooth, often

bright, rarely witty, and when *Lord Vauxhall*—who inherited no lands with his title—is made to say that this kinsman left him *vox et præterea nihil*, the patient hearer feels that the joke has been brought from far afield.

The good genius of the play, and especially of *Phryne*, is her cousin *Jack O'Beirne*, an Irish artist. Mr. Boucicault of course acts *O'Beirne*, and in the charming artistic fashion long so familiar. Never sounding the depths of either humour or pathos, Mr. Boucicault is yet exceedingly natural, graceful and sympathetic in both ; and he nowhere shows his art more convincingly than in the perfect facility with which he passes from one to the other. The inimitable *Kerry* was acted each evening before " Phryne," and the supporting company appeared to advantage in both plays.

" Cuisla-Ma-Chree," another new play by Mr. Boucicault—to the novelty of which, however, some exception must be made—was given for the first time on any stage at the Hollis Street Theatre, Boston, on the evening of Monday, February 20th. Several of this author-and-actor's most successful dramas, as the play-bill naïvely pointed out—among them " The Colleen Bawn," " Jeanie Deans," and " Rip Van Winkle "—have been " derived from novels previously employed with little or no effect by other dramatists." But " Cuisla-Ma-Chree " is scarcely an occasion for Mr. Boucicault to plume himself, as it follows substantially the story of the play which has long been familiar to the stage and keeps to Scott's romance with about the same closeness. Mr. Bouci-

cault uses a prologue for telling of the young heir's
abduction, and separates it by twenty years from the
following acts ; "otherwise"—as an accomplished
writer and critic of the theatre said of the first-night
performance—"his piece is little more than a substitution of Irish scenes, names, brogue and whisky for
Scotch, the shamrock for the thistle, the turf for the
heather." There is some loss, some gain, in the new
version. Much remains the same. Many passages,
like those in which *Julia Mannering* is serenaded by
her lover and *Meg Merrilies* sends the *Dominie* to the
rescue of *Harry Bertram*, are simply repeated. The
sibyl, whom two famous actresses, Charlotte Cushman
and Madame Janauschek, have impersonated—each
in her own great way—is turned into a generous,
passionate, but except for these qualities a very
commonplace old beggar-woman. Apart from the
queer changes of character, the chief fault of " Cuisla-
Ma-Chree " lies in its extreme length, slowness, and
heaviness ; it concentrates itself even less than the
old play of " Guy Mannering," and keeps at the same
time a similar dispersal of interest. The attack upon
the jail, introduced by Mr. Boucicault to give his
hero a prison-scene and rescue, has a sort of foundation
in the novel, and makes a tolerably effective scene on
the stage. As to the other characters, there is really
a taste of novelty in *Andy Dolan* and *Mollie* his wife.
Andy is a small farmer who begins life as a broth of
a boy ; he is somewhat sobered by marriage, but
remains to the end of the play the too-gallant and
too-generous being who appears in the pro'ogue.
Dandie Dinmont is of course the dramatic germ of

this character, although *Andy Dolan* becomes very different in idea. *Dr. Poldoodie* corresponds to *Dominie Sampson;* the "land agent" and villain to *Glosson; Barbara Coote* to *Julia Mannering;* and there are other resemblances which need not be named. The dialogue is neat and smooth—or it would not be Mr. Boucicault's—but it lacks the wit and point of many of the playwright's earlier compositions, and is quite without those quotable bits that are not infrequent even in a play so late among the author's efforts as "The Jilt."

The acting was better than the piece. Mr. Boucicault moved through the part of *Andy* with his own natural ease and grace, but showed no new phases of his talent ; and the character is not one to require the highest exercise of this actor's delightful skill. Mrs. Barker, in whom one finds the rather rare union of robust humour with a gift for detail, made a well-deserved hit as *Judy McCann, Andy's* warm-hearted aunt. Miss Eytinge acted the translated *Meg* in her more violent scenes with dry intensity, and struck the gentler notes of the character pleasantly if not with any great pathos ; Mr. Padgett deserves much commendation for the individual quality he contrived to impart to the character of *Dr. Poldoodie,* which must of course in its main lines follow that of Dominie Sampson ; and several of the other players earned good words. The very pretty scenery and the good acting helped out the heavy play, but many a spectator must have found his thought printed for him in the question of the clever critic who asked if it were "worth while to accept a tinsel *Meg* and a pinchbeck *Dominie Sampson* for the sake of seeing Mr. Boucicault in a diluted *Shaun* or *Conn.*"

But *Shaun* and *Conn*, and *Myles na Coppaleen*, too, were seen in their original form last season. "Arrah na Pogue," of which *Shaun* is the humble hero, was almost a novelty, as it had not been given before in several years. *Shaun* is one of those two or three types of Irish character which was brought to perfection in Mr. Boucicault's acting at a comparatively early stage of his career, and since that time—not to be too definitely fixed—he has played the same Celtic air with variations. Mr. Boucicault's beautiful and touching impersonation of *Kerry*, the faithful old butler—in which for once his pathos is without that suspicious facility which elsewhere attaches to it—is one of the most perfect things to be seen on our stage. But that stands by itself. Among Mr. Boucicault's other Irish characters two may perhaps be chosen as standing roughly for all the rest—*Conn* the *Shaughraun* and *Myles na Coppaleen* of " The Colleen Bawn." *Conn* is a light-hearted boy ; *Myles* makes an impression of greater maturity, and—along with the gay Celtic temperament—has a power of self-sacrifice and a reserve of steady purpose that is often thought of (it may be unjustly) as existing more frequently in other lands than in the land which wears the green. *Shaun* is the third of these best-known among Mr. Boucicault's earlier characters, and is much more nearly akin to *Myles* than to *Conn*. The rest seem for the most part repetitions and pleasant echoes of these. *Fin Mac Cool* is but the *Shaughraun* in

American clothes and an American environment, and *Andy Dolan*, and even *Myles O'Hara* and *Jack O'Beirne*, we have met before. In all these latest creations, too, Mr. Boucicault's acting is paler, less varied, less charming. It is less individual, it lacks spontaneity, and the same symbols are used too often. These comparisons are not made to be invidious, for nothing that Mr. Boucicault does is without many gracious touches which proclaim the artist; but it is desirable to acknowledge the fuller satisfaction to be found in his earlier impersonations. And one of the best of these is *Shaun the Post*. The mingled humour and pathos of the character are shown with unerring skill; and *Shaun's* devotion to the young master, the head of the Sept Mac-Cool, and the hope and trust in which he holds his *Arrah* are expressed with a charm that is not marred with a single false or careless touch. The faded green coat, the queer hat, and the red waistcoat, together make a picture which is the outward and visible sign of the *Shaun* who shares his grace and his mellow brogue with *Conn* and *Myles na Coppaleen*.

" The Jilt " was of course an important part of Mr. Boucicault's repertory last season, and formed the most attractive element in the copyright entertainment given at the Hollis Street Theatre on the afternoon of Wednesday, the 21st of March. Since this play was first seen there have been several good, if not brilliant, renderings by different companies of Mr. Boucicault's first noteworthy comedy (and, all things considered, his most noteworthy work) " London Assurance." And this is a good place for a word by way of com-

parison between two plays which have several points
in common. The traditions of older comedy survived
the hundred years and found a latter-day embodiment
in "London Assurance." The people of 1780 would
find themselves in sad perplexity before many of our
modern plays. They would be brought face to face
with standards of thought, speech and characterization of the most novel and surprising kind ; and the
opinions as well as the feelings of their descendants
could not fail, in more than one way, of seeming to
them uncommonly queer. But the author of "The
School for Scandal" might see "London Assurance"
and be persuaded that Richard Sheridan and Dion
Boucicault had many things in common. The persons
of the more modern drama do not wear wigs, or
patches, or small clothes, but the spectator may well
be surprised that they do not, for their conversation,
as well as their names, savours of a time when all those
things were worn, and snuff was taken into the bargain.
Sir Harcourt Courtly and his son pay elaborate com-
pliments, and *Grace Harkaway* and even *Lady Gay
Spanker* listen with as much complaisance as if they
were *Lydia Languish* or *Lady Betty Modish*. No-
body in the play, except *Dolly Spanker*, is incapable
of turning out antithesis or repartee, and much of the
talk has an unnatural finish and point. Inferior as is
"The Jilt" to "London Assurance" in most ways,
and especially in wit, compactness and address, one
cannot but be struck—on seeing the new play again
after a freshened recollection of the older one—with
Mr. Boucicault's advance in humanity of dialogue, so
to say, between the two. This advance almost makes

up for several imperfections that too readily disclose themselves. The plot rambles, and is sometimes a little difficult to follow ; somewhat too rough and too horsy a note is struck—if the expression may be permitted—for an English gentleman's house to-day, even though Budleigh Abbotts is in Yorkshire ; and the lapses of the dialogue into thinness sometimes make one sigh for less nature and more of the balanced wit of " London Assurance," which, if it was a palpable imitation, was also a palpable hit. But the plot has the one indispensable quality, that of sustained interest ; and the abundant incident and variety of character make " The Jilt " incomparably better than most modern plays.

The performance at the copyright benefit was probably as good as any that has been given since " The Jilt " was taken off the stage of the Boston Museum two years ago. Mr. Boucicault, is of course, easily first with his *Myles O'Hara*. His humour is irresistible, and his pathos, if it often seems a little *facile*, a little lacking in depth, is always genuine. *Myles O'Hara*, with his whimsical love for his horse Ballinahinch, his ready cheer, and his pathetic saying, " Misfortune is an epidemic in my country," will be longer remembered than any of the crowd of characters Mr. Boucicault has personated in the course of half a century, except *Kerry* and the three Irishmen of " The Colleen Bawn," The Shaughraun," and " Arrah-na-Pogue."

Several other Irish actors and plays demand a word. Chief among these, perhaps, is Mr. Joseph Murphy, whose *Kerry Gow* has long been familiar to

our stage.   Mr. Murphy appeared last season in
" The Donagh," a new romantic play written for him
by Mr. George Fawcett Rowe.   The piece does not
rise above the commonplace, and Mr. Murphy's supporting company was poor, but his own acting con-
tained, as ever, more than one passage of rough,
humorous worth.

Mr. J. C. Roach also offered a new play, which was
given at the Howard Athenæum on the 28th of
November.   " Dan Darcey " makes a weak attempt to
paint the life and fortunes of an Irishman in America,
but its plot is wildly melodramatic, and it has no
value as a picture of reality.   This play, however,
indicates a possible new departure, which Mr. Roach—
acting in some future and fitter drama—may be able
to make in earnest.   The Irish chronicle of the season, to be complete, needs but a slight reference to
Mr. Daniel Sully, the low comedian, and Mr. Scanlan,
the very good-looking young actor, who—after a
year's absence—entertained large audiences again with
" Shane-na-Lawn."

C. T. Copeland.

.

DOUBLE LIVES IN DRAMA.

No being, in real life or in the mimic life of the stage is absolutely single in purpose and motive, in affection or in expression. Any attempt to represent such a person is at once assigned to the category of the unacceptable improbabilities which the crude novelist or playwright attempts to foist off upon the inexperienced as proper representations of humanity. Not only are people actuated by many motives, governed by many principles, aud inspired by many desires, but in most persons these are so intertwined that it would be practically impossible to trace the actual consequence or influence of each in determining any particular resolve or action. Still there are to be perceived ruling loves, besetting sins and dominant principles in all strong specimens of the human race, and each of these is identified and remembered by these salient points of his character—the conditions which made them salient being, however, generally more internal and secret, and less traceable by observers and biographers.

One purpose of the stage is to show logically and in due sequence how various motives and circumstances affect people and produce from them the behaviour and the speech which carry on the story and work out its result. So far as these influences are exterior to a given personage, they are easily shown by the author's other puppets ; but so far as they are internal, they must be shown by the soliloquy, the aside, the by-play and the general suggestive power of the actor. Hence it is, that in such a play as " Hamlet," for instance, great stress is laid upon a correct delivery of the soliloquies, as best indicating the actor's conceptions of the character in its essence. So in " Othello," the test is applied to the manner in which *Iago* shows the various phases of his disposition and overlays his vengeful hate with smooth duplicity ; and yet again in " The Merchant of Venice," we depend upon *Shylock's* long aside in the third scene of the play for giving us the exact status of the personal relations and feelings existent between himself and the other Venetians. Not to multiply examples, it is easy to see that the business and the value of the stage lie in the exposition of this working upon one another of divers principles, and that he is accounted greatest among actors who can add to an ability for discriminating different personages by their prevalent elements, the higher ability to discriminate the elements which are merged and confused in the constitution of one person.

Often, however, the dramatist has felt that a stronger contrast and conflict of principles and elements can be shown, and more vivid stage effects produced, by dividing them between two individuals who, while having close physical likeness, have yet great spiritual opposition. From such there proceed plays like " The Lyons Mail," " The Corsican Brothers," and " Bleak House," in which one actor is required to represent alternately two essentially different persons. Plays in the course of which some personage is required to assume a disguise, seriously or to make fun for the spectator, are legion and not to be considered as embodying anything but expedients of action. It is only within a short time, however, that the stage has received a new idea—that of causing a single actor to represent antipodal extremes of character, embodied in forms also of opposing kinds and qualities. The novelist Stevenson drew in his short story, "Dr. Jekyll and Mr. Hyde," the outline of an absolutely dual life, in the course of which, when good prevailed, the man showed it in his acts, his words and in his ample and gracious person ; as, on the other hand, when evil predominated, his ugliness of speech and brutality of deed were concentrated in a shrunken, mis-shapen person. The unequal contest was waged through alternate possession of the man by this good and evil, rather than by their writhing, interlacing struggles, and when the end came it was in the absolute overthrow of the higher and purer principles and the extinction of the duplex existence in its degenerate and damning state.

This theme has been shown in dramatic form upon American stages, first by Mr. Richard Mansfield and second by Mr. Daniel E. Bandmann. Men of different physical and mental types, they approached the subject from different stand-points and developed from it different results. A comparison may easily be drawn between them, but it would be by no means easy to say which of the two creations was

really the greater, although there would be no difficulty for any spectator in deciding which better
suited his particular tastes and fancies.

Mr. Bandmann is an artist of long-tried talent,
educated in the careful German school, and eminent in
the early part of his career for his interpretation of
romantic but strongly-marked characters, as well as
for more than acceptable assumptions of the standard
tragic parts in Shakspere.. Of late years he has
been a wanderer in many countries, and in the
practice of his profession he has had to do some
commoner work which has brushed some of the
finesse from his style and weighted it with some
melodramatic manner.

Mr. Mansfield is a young man whose peculiar
talent seems sometimes to show almost a touch of
genius, but who has as yet only shown himself legi-
timately and directly powerful in a single part—the
Baron Chevrial in "A Parisian Romance." He is
a close student of effects, and there are many
minutiæ in his work which show judgment as well
as perception. He has an eye which sees below the
surface, and hence he is inclined to be too much
the diviner and so to be finical in his details.

The divergence between the two dramatizations
was fundamental. Mr. Bandmann, being a tall man
of rather handsome and agreeable presence, chose
to give full consequence to the large and genial
Jekyll; while Mr. Mansfield's slenderer build, for-
bidding him to attempt that, necessarily chose *Hyde*
as the principal feature of his play. This was to be
regretted, because, as the evil principle is the more

active and vital, it must necessarily have had pre-
dominance, even with a perfect *Jekyll*. In effect
Mr. Mansfield's *Jekyll* was a feeble, wishy-washy,
uninteresting and disintegrating creature, incapable
of any but a sickly resistance to temptation, while
Mr. Bandmann presented a strong, warm-hearted,
earnest man, whom it would not be easy to overcome,
and who would yield, not so much in woe as in
despairing fight, to devilish triumph, hoping against
hope and contesting every moment and every step
like doomed *Macbeth*.

In the representation of *Hyde* both actors had
similar notions, and it is to be said to their credit
that they used, as stage make-up goes, almost nothing
in the way of special appearances, although Mr.
Mansfield in particular has been charged with most
elaborate mechanical contrivances. A wig, with long
hair easily turned over the face or away from it, and
—in Mr. Bandmann's case—some contrivance for
covering the jaw so as to produce an effect of gaps
and tushes, and a frock-coat readily worn in
gentlemanly fashion, or huddled together in ruffianly
way, were about all. But both indulged in trickery
of lights and colours quite inconsistent with legitimate
development of effect, and at once deceptive and
distracting.

When Mr. N. C. Goodwin in some burlesque of
Mr. Irving said, " Now I am red with rage, and now
I turn green with jealousy," and had the correspond-
ing coloured lights turned upon him as he spoke,
everybody laughed as at a capital joke. The grim-
ness and the mystery of the *Hyde* situations—espe-

cially perplexing and at first inexplicable in the Mansfield version to those who did not know the story—depressed the spectator, and caused him to accept a sudden change from the rose, the yellow and the grey of sunlight, twilight or lamplight, to the hideous mockery of stage green, or the instant and irrational dusk, which almost invariably accompanied the apparition of *Hyde*. The death-scene was kept in larger and freer light and air by Mr. Mansfield, as in that the transformation is scarcely more than hinted at, as the victim of his own folly and crime hides the dying features over which he feels the awful shadow is coming.

Of the two impersonations, Mr. Mansfield's was the subtler, the more instinct with a devilish *daimon*, and Mr. Bandmann's was more coarse and rough and low in overt action, gloating with snarls and inarticulate noises over the iniquities which Mr. Mansfield's wretch perpetrates as if by an independent inspiration. Mr. Bandmann's gained by the relief afforded by his *Jekyll*, but it lost by a clap-trap apotheosis of the ransomed sinner which followed upon the *dénouement*.

Each play added to the original a love episode to soften and set off the domestic disposition of *Jekyll*; but Mr. Mansfield's plan would not, for reasons already intimated, allow this to be so well developed as Mr. Bandmann's. On the other hand, Mr. Mansfield introduced a distinct creation in the old, crabbed, miserly and half-crazed keeper of the lodging occupied by *Hyde*. Each of the dual impersonations was a definite contribution, possessing real value, to the stage, and although each appealed to, and was generally patronized by, a different audience—Mr. Mansfield's being perhaps the more select and Mr. Bandmann's the more "popular"—each ought to have been seen and found interesting and good by the admirers of the other, as in each the judgment of the critics marked for approval evidences of earnest thought and genuine art earnestly and forcibly applied to a difficult and even dangerous subject.

HOWARD MALCOM TICKNOR.

MISS MORRIS IN "RENÉE DE MORAY."

MR. CLINTON STUART'S adaptation of M. D'Ennery's
"La Martyre" was given for the first time on the
evening of January 9th, at the Globe Theatre,
Boston, with Miss Clara Morris in the character of
the unhappy wife. The play was afterwards acted
in New York, and has met with great success. It
would be unprofitable to enter upon any comparison
between "The Martyr," the version of the French
played at the Madison Square Theatre, and the
adaptation made by Mr. Stuart. Suffice it to say
that the action of "Renée de Moray," as it now stands,
begins on the piazza of an hotel at Aix-les-Bains,
where *Madame de Moray* is surprised and shocked to
receive a visit from a brother of whose existence
she has until then been ignorant—*Claude Burel*, the
illegitimate son of her mother, *Madame de la Marche*.
Renée (*Mdme. de Moray*) has the deepest love and
respect for her mother ; she insists that *Claude* shall
not make his existence known to her, and rather than
have her mother endure the mortification of knowing
that her guilty secret has been told—above all, to
keep it from reaching the ears of the *Comte de Moray*,
and perhaps the world at large—*Renée* agrees to
meet *Claude* in Paris, whither she and her husband
the count are going, and make over to him the sum

Q

of 100,000 francs, which he demands. Several days
go by, and *Claude*, becoming impatient while his
sister is negotiating for the sale of her jewels, presents
himself in her apartments. During his visit the
money is sent in from the jeweller, but before this
Mdme. de la Marche enters, and *Claude* is so touched
by her appearance and kind words that, after she
goes away, he is unwilling to accept money for the
compromising letters in his possession; *Renée* presses
it upon him with affectionate protestations; and the
Comte de Moray enters to find the brother and sister
in each other's arms. It is easy to see the difficulty
and the dramatic promise of such a situation.
Moray's mind has already been poisoned by one
Palmeri, a super-subtle Neapolitan, and he is ready to
believe that *Claude* is *Renée's* lover. When at length
he threatens to shoot *Claude* if he does not give up
the letters—themselves an apparent evidence of guilt
—the unhappy woman is on the point of telling the
whole truth, but her mother enters at this moment
and *Renée's* lips are sealed. The count fires, *Claude*
falls dead, and *Renée* replies to every question,
"Yes, the dead man loved me." The dramatic force
of all this emphatic grouping is beyond a shadow of
doubt, and the ethical aspect of *Renée's* course may
be left to take care of itself; but the startled beholder,
when he has—as it were—eluded the grasp of the
scene, begins to ask himself whether a woman of
mature years would have considered her erring
mother so much and have had so little compunction
for the husband and child who, in the matter at
stake, were without sin. And this is yielding

nothing to the human selfishness and weakness which would naturally move a woman to save herself, but granting everything to the exalted nature of *Renée*. The question may pend, but the reader must be reminded that this really tremendous situation—the most vivid and most important in the play—comes at the end of the second act, and that three acts remain to be played. It is no small tribute to the quality of Mr. Stuart's material and his skill in using it to say that the almost inevitable anti climax is treated with great discretion ; the gentle decline in interest becomes distinctly an ascension in the fourth act, and incidents and persons are combined and distributed with so much cleverness that, from the beginning to the end of the piece, the spectator's attention is seldom allowed to wander. The tale shall be unfolded no more than to say that *Renée* does not die, that *Mdme. de la Marche* herself clears her daughter's name, and that *Palmeri's* sister, the duchess—whom *Moray* has married, after divorcing *Renée*—turns out to be a *duchesse à rire*. The one general fault which must impress even people whose emotions are most responsive, lies in the fact that the instances of self-sacrifice—of which not a tithe has been told—are needlessly multiplied, and that, to be brief, the agony is too long drawn out.

The pathetic interest of this play centres, of course, in *Renée de Moray*, and the part is in many ways singularly adapted to Miss Morris's unequal genius. Her genius and its inequality have long been so well known that no more is necessary to be said of Miss Morris's *Renée* than that much of it is done in her best manner. Up to the end of the second act Miss Morris played throughout with almost uninterrupted power and truth, and in the last scene of this act she stood over the body of the murdered man in a reality of grief and horror that passed the limit of interest and excitement and became appalling. In later scenes Miss Morris more often lost her hold of the part in that curious and disappointing way which seems an indispensable condition of her acting, and her most distressing faults were all present in the exaggeration and even rant of much of the passionate scene with *Moray*. But even in episodes where Miss Morris is at her worst, those who are familiar with her impersonations well know how the drawl gives way most unexpectedly to a tense utterance of grief or passion, and how some meaningless waste of words is suddenly lighted with a flash of insight or comprehension that leaves the spectator dazzled with its brilliancy.

Mr. Graham, Miss Morris's leading man, is one of those actors who—in spite of effective episodes—seem destined to remain always in the rough. Mrs. Allen and Mr. Clarges played with veteran competence and certainty, and with only a qualified resemblance to life. The others vibrated diversely between honesty and carelessness, between crudeness and the painfully theatrical. It should, however, be recorded that the young lady who played *Renée's* daughter was often delightfully fresh and natural.

C. T. COPELAND.

MR. FREDERICK WARDE.

THE part of *Virginius* in Sheridan Knowles's well-known tragedy was chosen by Mr. Frederick Warde for his first appearance in Boston in a leading character. The performance was first witnessed at the Hollis Street Theatre on the evening of November 28th, 1887, by an audience fair in numbers and enthusiastic in approval, and it is pleasant to add that Mr. Warde's acting more than once justified the approval. The part of *Virginius* was handed on from Forrest to McCullough, and since the death of that lamented actor it has been, as it were, in abeyance ; so that one who would now attempt "the high Roman fashion" has to contend against the memory of the dead, often more formidable than the rivalry of the living. Mr. Warde has some good gifts of his own. Of the middle weight and size, he is erect and well made ; dignity of carriage and a great variety of gestures—often too great, indeed—give him advantages in playing tragedy ; a grave, expressive face and very brilliant dark eyes are still further in Mr. Warde's favour. His voice is far too throaty, and his enunciation—although admirably distinct and intelligent—suffers from an almost constant exaggeration of the consonants. Mr. Warde uses his arms rather stiffly, and this and the profusion of gesture already spoken of have their parallels in a general stiffness and elaboration of method. It will readily be seen that in applying such a method to a part so highly conventionalized as *Virginius* – of which Mr. Warde's conception is nearly one with that already familiar to us—the result must often be sadly artificial. Partly also from such a system must come the too marked transitions from one emotion to another, and the exaggerated expression of grief, rage or pride, which are too often exhibited in Mr. Warde's acting. But that would be a narrow judgment indeed, which, on account of these formal defects—many and great though they be—should fail to recognize Mr. Warde's grasp of the character, his absolute sincerity, and his dramatic force at critical situations. When the emotion is complex, as when *Virginius* is divided among so many different thoughts and desires in listening to the evil tidings brought by *Lucius*, Mr. Warde is most artificial and accordingly least successful. But when he is determined to be gone, action is suited to word, and the effect upon the spectator is real and direct. Earlier in the scene, the expression of grief over *Dentatus;* the passionate appeals to the gods ; the furious attack on *Caius Claudius* in the forum, the appeal to the citizens, and the killing of *Virginia ;*—all these make a quick appeal to the on-looker. Mr. Warde's indications of insanity alternated pretty evenly between good and bad, but he showed true artistic feeling in making the hero's last moments brief and entirely simple.

In the supporting company, Mr. Rand led the others in professional skill and competence ; many deserve a good word, and Mr. Handyside, Mr. Edwards, and Mr. Stuart—as *Icilius*, *Caius Claudius* and *Lucius*—deserve especial praise for their honest and earnest work. The stage management was unintelligent, and the lictors and other armed men unnecessarily lop-sided ; but one or two good effects were produced in grouping, and the march down from the hills with the dead body of *Dentatus*, followed and preceded by the Roman eagles, was really impressive. It must be said that the performance, as a whole, gave an impression of exaggeration, often of crudeness, and very often of too much noise. Mr. Warde also appeared during the season in " Damon and Pythias," in a version of " The Gladiator," and in a new romantic play called "Gaston Cadol." This drama, as to the origin of which no information was given save that it was adapted from the French by Miss Celia Logan, has some merit, and was received with favour. It remains to be seen whether it will keep the stage. Mr. Warde's acting in all these plays had much the same merits and defects that disclosed themselves in " Virginius," and—if never highly satisfactory—was always made interesting by its earnestness and manliness.

C. T. COPELAND.

ENGLISH COMEDY BY MISS VOKES.

THAT charming English actress, Miss Rosina Vokes, spent the entire season of 1887-88 in the United States, appearing in all the principal cities and in many of the smaller towns. Among the more notable features of her tour were long engagements in San Francisco, Chicago, Boston, and New York (Miss Vokes played a number of weeks in the last-named city at Daly's Theatre, beginning April 16th, and remained at the Park Theatre in Boston three weeks in the December previous), and visits of a single week to Jersey City, Philadelphia (unfortunately interrupted by illness), Baltimore and other places. Miss Vokes's company was one of exceptional excellence, comparing favourably with that of the previous season, although, with the exception of Mr. Thorpe and Miss Irving, none of the members had been with Miss Vokes before. Of these new members, Mr. Morton Selten was immediately recognized by competent critics as an exceptionally clever actor with a thoroughly brisk, facile and constantly refined touch ; Miss Ethel Johnson, a young lady with a beautifully modulated voice and a singular charm of manner, made a favourable impression ; Mr. Felix Morris, a distinctively "character" actor, did one or two things admirably and others less well ; and Mr. F. Gottschalk displayed a quiet, sincere and natural style which was very pleasing. The plays presented during the season were as follows : " The Widow's Device," "The Circus Rider," " Which is Which ? " " Cousin Zachary " (all new), and " In Honour Bound," " My Milliner's Bill," " A Pantomime Rehearsal," " A Double Lesson " (given in previous seasons). Brief criticisms of the plays and the manner of their performance follow.

" The Widow's Device " is an older play re-written and re-named ; and those who have ever read or witnessed " A Lesson in Love " will have no difficulty in tracing its paternity. Briefly described, it · is a comedy of intrigue (using the phrase in its distinctive sense) the interest of which depends almost wholly upon the cleverness of its situations. Although it naturally reaches a higher dramatic level than the so-called farce-comedy, pure and simple, it is not by any means a favourable specimen of its class. In point of delicacy and cleverness it is not to be compared with similar plays of the French school. The dialogue never reaches the distinction of brilliancy, and the wit is of the moderately amusing order. Some of the entanglements into which the characters fall are rather well managed ; but, generally speaking, the humour of the situations depends largely upon the efforts of the actors. The story is simply that of a fascinating widow who endeavours to help an old friend to a charming young wife in the person of a pretty heiress whom another gentleman is also anxious to win. An offensive and defensive alliance against this obnoxious suitor is formed between the two ; but the plan is foiled alike by the awkwardness of the man and by his final discovery that he is really in love with the widow. The unnamed author of the comedy, however, is so plainly unequal to the opportunities of such a situation that one wishes, long before the problem is finally solved, for some such clever hand as that of M. Scribe to relieve the situation with the irradiating flash of genuine wit. The company are not very seriously tried by the demands of the piece. Miss Vokes is not at her best as the widow ; what she lacks most of all, perhaps, is a certain distinction of manner that the part imperatively demands. Of course she has moments which are vivid with her rare personal charm and her piquant and delightful humour ; the country dance at the end of the first act is one such moment. The burden and heat of the play is fairly borne by Mr. Morton Selten, who is thoroughly entertaining in his impersonation of *Orlando Middlemark*, the finally successful suitor of the heiress. His agreeable presence and his finished dramatic method do him yeoman's service ; and whatever interest the game of cross purposes possesses is largely due to him. His byplay is highly amusing, and it keeps, besides, within the purely humorous and does not descend to the merely grotesque. This, we need hardly add, is praise that can seldom be accorded in these degenerate days of horse-play and buffoonery. Mr. Thorpe is not particularly felicitous as the bashful lover ; indeed, he makes the ingenuous East Indian colonel a good deal of a ninny, if not an absolute

milksop.   For our own part, we seldom care for his
acting except when he has the task of portraying
quiet emotion.   Mr. Felix Morris, in the character of
an old gossip who is three parts cad and one part
mischief-maker, is rather amusing, and Mesdames
Stafford and Irving deserve a word of moderate
commendation.

"The Circus Rider," by Mrs. Charles Doremus, is
a charming comedy in one act, particularly adapted
to the abilities of Miss Vokes.   The plot is ingenious,
and turns upon the attempt of *Lord Weldon,* who is
affianced to *Lady Lucille Grafton,* to contrive an
accident by which the carriage of a circus-rider for
whom he has a penchant shall be overturned near
his house and the occupant compelled perforce to sup
with him.   But it turns out that his *fiancée* meets
with the mishap intended for the other flame, and
so has a chance, not only to learn of her lover's
perfidy, but to find what promises to be another lover
in the person of the friend whom *Lord Weldon* has
left to entertain his guest.   Miss Vokes does some
delightful acting as the supposed circus-rider, better in
its humour than in its pathos ; and her clever imitation
of "the great Montebella's famous bare-backed act "
—out of keeping with the character of an English
lady as it is—is invariably received with the highest
enthusiasm by the audience.   Mr. Selten shows a fine
quality of artistic reserve in an unsympathetic part,
and Mr. Gottschalk's impersonation of the Butler is
in every way admirable.   Mr. Thorpe is rather uninteresting as *Lord Weldon.*

"Which is Which ?" is a delightful little farce, with

just that touch of pathos which gives even absurdity the appearance of reality. It concerns a young artist desperately in debt and the two girls, one an heiress and the other a companion, whom his eccentric old uncle brings to his studio. He is man enough to imitate Mr. Gilbert's hero in following his heart's dictates, and so he makes love to the pretty companion, who turns out to be the heiress after all. The piece is skilfully played. Mr. Selten is admirable as the artist, and Mr. Felix Morris almost equally so as the choleric old uncle. Miss Ethel Johnson is very sweet and winning as the pseudo-companion.

"A Game of Cards" is more pathetic than humorous. It concerns the quarrel of two old men over the game which gives a name to the piece—a quarrel which very nearly wrecked the happiness of two lovers. Mr. Morris plays a choleric old nobleman with some success, and Mr. Selten does excellent work as the young lover.

"Cousin Zachary," another one-act play, also keeps more nearly to pathos than to humour. The central theme of the piece, *Zachary's* sacrifice of his own feelings towards his ward in order that she may marry the young artist to whom he finds her heart is given, is by no means new, of course, although it so far partakes of the eternal in mankind as to be perpetually vivid and impressive. But the idea is rather crudely and hastily worked out. The skill of the author is insufficient to satisfy the demands which he makes upon the emotions of the spectator, and the abrupt transitions from grave to gay do not reach the sources either of honest tears or of genuine

lau_hter. The piece is well acted by Mr. Morris,
Mr. Selten and Miss Johnson. Mr. Morris gives
Cousin Zachary a certain honest eloquence of feeling,
without at all penetrating into the regions of delicate
and exquisite art. Mr. Selten does very well the
little which is demanded of him, and Miss Johnson
plays with grace and feeling another rather colourless
part.

The plays which have been done by Miss Vokes in
previous years require no especial mention here.

EDITOR.

"A POSSIBLE CASE."

THE divorce laws of the United States are as interesting in one sense as they are iniquitous in another; interesting because they give rise to singular and dramatic complications; iniquitous because such complications are necessarily immoral. A man, for example, with an honest and faithful wife in New York, may swear falsely to that wife's dishonour in Illinois, and, without her knowledge or consent, divorce himself from her in the latter State. To cap the climax of indecent absurdity, a man residing in New York may have several living wives, each wife being legally bound to him by the laws of the State in which they married. In view of these facts, which stand for one of the most serious vices that confront our civilization, it is surprising that American dramatists and novelists have failed to give much attention to them. Our divorce laws would certainly offer but a feeble defence against really powerful satire. We possess the laws, unfortunately, and lack the satire. Who shall write for us another "Uncle Tom's Cabin," directed, not at the slavery of the human body, but at the slavery of the marriage contract?

An attempt was made recently to use our divorce laws as the basis for a novel. This novel is properly entitled "It is the Law," and, though an achievement of the slightest literary worth, it puts before us a great deal of unpleasant truth in compact form. It is quite likely that Mr. Sydney Rosenfeld, a clever young dramatist, found in this novel ideas for his play, " A Possible Case," which has been successfully acted in New York during the last few weeks, and which has, on the whole, been accounted an amusing and intelligent piece. I cannot say, of my own knowledge, however, that Mr. Rosenfeld is acquainted with " It is the Law." But the coincidence of a novel and a play dealing with a single and unusual subject is, at least, striking. It should be admitted without hesitation that the play is decidedly a brighter thing than the novel.

" A Possible Case," as every one knows, was written for the Union Square Theatre, and was to have followed Mr. Bronson Howard's lively farce, " The Henrietta," there. The theatre was suddenly destroyed by fire, and Mr. Rosenfeld's play had its first production in Brooklyn. It was afterwards presented in three New York threatres, and, as these lines are being written, is still on the stage of the Madison Square Theatre. The piece has, therefore, passed through an exceptional experience, and it has certainly weathered vicissitudes which might easily have ruined another work. Moreover, wherever it has been seen, it has aroused much favourable comment and applause. It may, then, be justly spoken of as a creditable addition to the rather short list of new American plays.

In " A Possible Case " Mr. Rosenfeld has, evidently, two objects : his first object is to show just what the American divorce laws are, and to cast the light of

ridicule upon them ; his second object is to tell a story,
more or less comic, built upon these laws, and to
answer the question how a wife with three husbands
on her hands may finally assume the dignified and
moral position of a wife with a single husband. He
has succeeded tolerably well in both his objects, but
by no means entirely well. The position of his heroine
in the play comes very close to indelicacy ; it is, surely,
far from agreeable to look upon a pretty woman who
has actually lived with three men, all of them still in
the best of health, even if the three men are supposed
to be her legal husbands. The manner in which this
complex matrimonial problem is finally straightened
out is, however, ingenious, and it is in a spirited vein
of comedy. One of the husbands has been guilty of
crime, and, by the laws of the state in which he
married, the committing of a crime dissolves wedlock ;
a second husband is released from his contract by the
unexpected appearance on the scene of a former wife ;
the third husband—the youngest, handsomest, and
most sympathetic—is thus left the sole possessor of
the woman. The play reaches a felicitous end ; but
its indirect value—its greatest value, indeed—lies in
the suggestion of a possible case which might not
have so happy a solution.

The story of " A Possible Case " is partially out-
lined in what has just been said. The heroine, *Mrs.
Mendoza,* is, presumably, a young widow. In the belief
that she is a widow, she marries *Laurence Gould.* The
latter is unfortunate enough to be mistaken for *Mendoza*
by a gang of sailor-detectives, and, as these persons desire to capture *Mendoza,* they manage to capture *Gould.*

He is gagged and borne away, and, soon afterwards, *Mrs. Mendoza* esteems herself a widow. As a widow she is courted by *Mr. Brinkerhoff*, a fat gentleman of means, and by *Allen Weeks*, a lean gentleman without means. The former is successful, and *Mrs. Mendoza* becomes *Mrs. Brinkerhoff*. By one of those queer turns of fate which the dramatist is always glad to make use of, even to the last stretch of improbability, both *Gould* and *Mendoza* turn up suddenly in *Brinkerhoff's* home. The rest of the play is simply a process of disentanglement, in which the American divorce laws are exposed for the benefit of the American public, the result being as I have indicated —Mrs. Mendoza-Gould-Brinkerhoff's release from her tripartite alliance.

It can hardly be said for Mr. Rosenfeld that he has got out of his subject all that might be got out of it. In the first place, his method of work is somewhat indefinite. One cannot be certain whether he means to be serious or merely flippant. His play touches occasionally upon drama ; then it goes off on a tangent of extreme farce. Drama and farce make a poor combination in any case, and not less so in "A Possible Case." But Mr. Rosenfeld deserves credit for having written a play which has decisive and novel elements of interest, which is in many respects cleverly handled, and which is rather aggressively American.

GEORGE EDGAR MONTGOMERY.

R

MR. SOTHERN'S FIRST TOUR.

"THE Highest Bidder," a play which came to New
York early in the year with much *prestige* of
success from London, was equally successful in
Boston and in other cities during the season of
1887-88. Mr. E. H. Sothern played *Jack Hammerton*,
and the other parts were taken by members of the
Lyceum Theatre Company. The play opens in right
English fashion; breakfast is laid at "The Larches,"
Mr. Lawrence Thornhill's place in Kent; presently
there enters to the butler *Mr. Bonham Cheviot* of
"The Firs," a neighbour of *Thornhill's;* then *Thornhill* himself, and before long *Jack Hammerton*, of
Hammerton, Mallet & Co., London, who may be
described as genteel auctioneers. This young fellow
is not intended by the playwrights to be entirely a
gentleman by birth and training, but he has what are
often called gentlemanly instincts, and eminently he
has what Lord Tennyson used to think better than
coronets and all that sort of thing. *Hammerton* is in
much grief for his friend—who had once done his
father a kindness—because *Thornhill's* affairs are in
sad case, and "The Larches" must be sold at auction.
His sympathy is still more poignant because he loves
Rose, Thornhill's pretty daughter, who now comes in
from the garden to breakfast with *Mrs. Honiton Lacy*

and her daughter. They are both staying at the house, and so likewise is *Sir Muffin Struggles*, a philanthropist, who comes down very late indeed. Yet another guest is *Sir Evelyn Graine*, a well-born blackleg, and he and his villainies are the hinges of the plot. *Hammerton* warns *Rose* against him, but only incurs her displeasure, because at the moment he lacks proof for his charges; and through *Sir Evelyn's* wicked presence of mind, and the later discovery that, although *Mr. Thornhill* is ruined, *Rose* will still have a dowry, *Hammerton* fails to make it clear that the shady baronet wished to marry her only for her fortune. In the next act, however— theatrical time is measured so differently from time at large—at the auction salesroom, where *Mr. Thornhill* and his daughter have come to attend the sale of their own estate, a despatch intended for *Sir Evelyn* comes into the hands of *Hammerton*. This announces that the horse he had backed has been beaten, and that his "only hope" is "the heiress." Now, of course, *Jack* has the baronet on the hip. But the advantage is fleeting, for the *Thornhills* are still further offended because he knocks down "The Larches" to a Jew, and they fail to understand that this is only an agent who is bidding it in for *Hammerton* himself. The rising curtain clears up the matter again in the third and last act, but again only for a moment. *Hammerton* generously makes over the title-deeds to *Thornhill*, but offers himself to *Rose*, as if she were mere value received for "The Larches," and things are now very bad indeed. The dramatic scheme of "The Highest Bidder" is droll in this, that no sooner do things begin to get a little better for the hero than they at once become a little worse; but after each gain and each loss a slight preponderance of gain remains to *Hammerton*. These successive advances and relapses will remind the arithmetical reader of the frog coming out of the well, but no play-going reader need be told that the feat is accomplished at last and that *Hammerton* comes out into the light and air of prosperity. The sub-plot is cared for by *Mrs. Honiton Lacy* and her designs on *Sir Muffin*; and by *Louisa* her daughter and one *Wiggins, Hammerton's* clerk, who run away together in the third act. "The Highest Bidder," as this hint of its outline has perhaps suggested, is an old-fashioned farcical comedy, conventional in its main lines, but with some elements of novelty in the scene at the auction-rooms. The dialogue, although it contains a small number of good jokes, is also the kind of thing which has been heard very often; but plenty of action, and a constant succession of scenes that are cleverly adapted to the stage, give the play a rattling sort of interest, and keep the spectator's attention to the end.

Mr. E. H. Sothern, who takes the chief part in "The Highest Bidder," is—besides being the son of an admired father—one of two or three young Englishmen who have graced our stage within the past few years, and, by their good breeding, manner, and bearing, have gained the favourable regard of the best sort of theatre-goers. Mr. Sothern won golden opinions here in his part of the English officer in "One of Our Girls," where it was necessary for him

to enact simply a very manly and rather diffident
young fellow. But every one who has been in the
least an observer of acting knows how hard it is to
make an illusion of entire simplicity and straight-
forwardness, of single-heartedness and an utter
absence of affectation. This illusion, it is not too
much to say, was compassed by Mr. Sothern in the
character he undertook in Mr. Bronson Howard's
comedy ; and the light touch and sincere method
which served him so well there have been even more
for Mr. Sothern's advantage in " The Highest Bidder."
For *Jack Hammerton* is a constant exaggeration ;
he touches life, to be sure, but touches it, one may
say, only to rebound into farce ; and very natural
acting is required to keep the part within the limits of
belief. *Hammerton's* most obvious characteristic is
the wildest diffidence and confusion in the company
of women, but his head is level by nature, and his
heart is always in the right place. When there are
only men to deal with he can, if need be, show himself both wise and determined, but on all ordinary
occasions *Hammerton* says the thing that one would
rather not have said, and in correcting himself is
capable of saying any number of the same sort of
thing. All this is very skilfully indicated by Mr.
Sothern, whose tones, gestures, glances, and—above
all—laugh, are models of embarrassment. But the
same symbols are used too often, the last scene of
shy wooing is palpably too long, and the suggestion
keeps making itself that even *Jack Hammerton* would
have had more lucid moments in which to let his true
character shine out. Whenever the real *Hammerton*

does appear, no one who has seen Mr. Sothern needs to be told how sweet and fine and true—and withal how manly—is his acting. Among the supporting players, only one, Mr. C. B. Bishop, can be singled out for much praise. His *Bonham Cheviot*, a variation of Boythorne, is a thoroughly delightful performance. The choleric temper and the kind heart, the rough speech and gentle thoughts of such a man have seldom been better represented on the stage ; and Mr. Bishop—who showed *Cheviot* equally well in his raving over trifles and his generosity in essence—won a deserved triumph from the audience. Of the other players, Miss Archer drags in her method, and is wonderfully undramatic when she ought to be most dramatic ; Miss Mowbray and Miss Friend, who played *Mrs. Lacy* and her daughter, are dryly competent, and no more than this is to be said for the rest. A certain hardness and loudness in the general tone of the performance—from which even Mr. Sothern does not always escape—probably comes from much acting of the same thing.

It is a sufficient index of the present condition of taste that the demand for " The Highest Bidder " in American cities and towns was so great, that Mr. Sothern did not feel himself warranted in giving it up for a new play ; and accordingly this trite, dreary piece occupied the whole of his return engagement in Boston, which began on the 14th of May and lasted two weeks. The only change in the cast was the substitution of Miss Fanny Addison for Miss Mowbray in the part of *Mrs. Honiton Lacy,* and the performances were smooth and hard.

During this second engagement " Editha's Burglar," which had been seen here with " The Great Pink Pearl," was given before " The Highest Bidder" at every performance. This Arcadian little sketch of Mrs. Burnett's is one of the very few plays in which a child is the "star," and the part of *Editha* would be dreary enough in the hands of most stage children. But little Elsie is not a stage-child—that compound of doll and parrot which sets the teeth of the judicious on edge. She is a fairy, with both smiles and tears at her command. Mr. Sothern, as *Bill Lewis*, is more gentle and refined than the ideal burglar would be, but he shows at one or two points emotional power of a kind for which his other parts have given no opportunity. It is safe to predict a brilliant future for this young and well-graced actor, unless indeed it should befall him to play such parts as *Jack Hammerton* until his style becomes hopelessly stiff and mannered.

C. T. COPELAND.

SOME MINOR PLAYS.

To attempt even to enumerate the plays brought
forward during the dramatic season of 1887-88, and
at the same time to give each one serious critical consideration, would extend this volume far beyond the
limits proposed. The more important productions
have already been considered with some fu'ness, and
many of the less important ones have received sufficient attention in the opening article by another
writer. Although they have given us nothing in the
way of novelty, it would be ungracious to let the
opportunity go by of saying a word as to Mr. Joseph
Jefferson, as well as to Mr. William J. Florence and
his amiable wife. The first-named is perhaps the
greater artist ; certainly he has the finer and the
keener method. This fact leads one naturally to
regret that he should devote himself exclusively to
" Rip Van Winkle," " The Cricket on the Hearth "
and " Lend Me Five Shillings," though each one of
these plays shows him in a distinct and admirable
light. To point out the characteristics of his art,
therefore, to a public which knows each one of these
so well, would be entirely superfluous. Nor is Mr.
Florence less well known. We have placed him
below Mr. Jefferson as an artist ; but the distinction
only holds good, perhaps, as regards method and not

as regards inspiration. Much of his work has unfortunately been in the domain of farce rather than comedy; his *Bardwell Slote*, good as it is, must be placed chiefly within the former category. But when Mr. Florence attempts comedy pure and simple how admirable in freshness and fervour he often is! Where shall we look for a truer and more exquisite impersonation than his *Cap'n Cuttle*, with his delicious repetition of faith in *Bunsby*, "If any man kin, he kin," and his chromatic scale of emotions upon the simple question, "Drown'ded, ain't he?" by which he tells *Florence Dombey* of *Walter's* safe return?

Unfortunately few of the minor plays or the players who interpret them deserve the respect which the great artists we have named have fairly earned by years of labour upon the stage. Indeed, the chief part of what the public is called upon to endure (and it apparently likes the task) is quite beneath criticism and almost beneath contempt. One of those to whom no such harsh strictures fairly apply, however, is Miss Lotta, who this year brought forward a new play, "Pawn Ticket 210," hardly so good as the more familiar pieces in which every one has learned to like her. This new work of Messrs. Greene and Belasco is a grotesque mess of absurdities, in which whatever is funny is (for the most part) not new, and whatever is new is in the main anything but funny. Indeed the "chestnut bell" might have been used to ring down the drop-curtain on more than one scene. The opening situations form an exception. They are droll, and have also a savour of novelty; for, unless in some old and dimly re-

membered farce a girl has been put in pawn and a
ticket taken out for her in the regular way, this idea
is new to our stage. *Uncle Harris's* pawn-shop was
cleverly set, with its watches and brass candlesticks,
its "Martha Washington Chair" and odd bits of
uniform suggesting army and navy revels to the
spectator; and the first scene was played with a
good deal of grotesque drollery. But the notion
of the pawned girl is used little or not at all for
mirthful purposes; it is rather made the turning
point in a stunning plot of the good old school;
and if that fortunate youth, the old play-goer, has
Miss Lotta's acting well in mind, he can figure to
himself the really *bizarre* effect obtained by grafting
her acting upon such a plot. Miss Lotta, in fact,
is a constant reminiscence of her familiar performances in other plays, and is by no means without
clever turns, flashes of humour and swift, dry retorts,
that are all three excellent of their kind. But Miss
Lotta's acts and words are for the most part very
unreal farce, and both these and the new part in
which they are now exhibited are untruthful farce.
They are in a sort of parallel line with life, and so
never touch it. The same statement – with a
difference which we shall endeavour to make manifest—may apply to Mr. N. C. Goodwin, who took up
Mr. Jefferson's part in "Lend Me Five Shillings,"
and also produced a new play, "Turned Up," during
this same season. In "Lend Me Five Shillings,"
Mr. Goodwin of course takes the character of *Mr.
Golightly.* Great pains have been employed to inform
the public that the younger actor has never seen

either Mr. Warren or Mr. Jefferson in the part, and
that his conception of it is therefore entirely an
original one. The statement is something of a *non
sequitur*, though for once we are willing to admit its
essential truth. Mr. Goodwin's impersonation is all
his own, and long may it remain so. Once grant the
possibility of the actor's dramatic method, and his
acting is tolerably amusing ; but such a concession
is exactly what no person of taste ought to be willing
to make. Mr. Goodwin is a master of mummery
and grimace, and he even has a sort of comic force ;
but he seems to have precisely that idea of the serious
principles of art which one usually expects to find
on the variety stage. The most that can be said for
his *Mr. Golightly* is that it does not offend actively
in the familiar line of mere buffoonery which we have
learned to expect from Mr. Goodwin, and that at
times his rather marvellous power of facial control is
responsible for some really humorous effects. But a
comparison with the artistic work of Mr. Jefferson in
the same part is as foolish as putting a gaudy chromo
beside the canvas of a great master. In "Turned
Up," which is a so-called "farcical comedy" of the
familiar pattern, Mr. Goodwin shows to much better
advantage than in "Lend Me Five Shillings." The
story of the piece revolves about a singular complication, involving apparent bigamy for a husband and
wife apparently separated by the death of the former.
The majority of the characters are riotous impossibilities indeed, though in one or two instances clever
acting gives them a semblance of humanity. Mr.
Goodwin, as *Caraway Bones, Esq.*, an undertaker, has
moments of real comic force. His drunken scene in

the second act, for instance, is rather well done, and with much less exuberance than we are accustomed to see from him. His make-up is humorous in itself, and in several odd moments through the play his acting deserves the same adjective. But the impersonation is not, all things considered, an especially effective one. Mr. Mason made a very good showing with the much-harassed *George Medway ;* Mr. Coote's vacuous laugh gave his *Ned Steddan* a degree of interest ; and Mr. T. H. Burns did some excellent work as *Captain Medway.* The young women of the company were unpleasantly nasal in their efforts to make themselves heard, and shared with the men the fault of roaring like bulls of Bashan upon the slightest provocation.

The pieces of Mr. Charles H. Hoyt, of which we have already had enough and much more than enough, along with others obviously built upon the same model, were produced with great abundance during the past season. "A Tin Soldier," "A Rag Baby" and all the more familiar examples of Hoytism continued to enjoy immense vogue in various parts of the country ; and even the contemptible idiocies of Mr. Hoyt's last piece, "A Hole in the Ground," did not disgust his admirers. The scene of this vulgar variety-show is laid in a railway station, and the humours of the "baggage-smasher" and "the *lady* of the lunch-counter" are brought into constant requisition. Beyond one or two touches of broad satire concerning the conduct of American railway officials, "A Hole in the Ground" has nothing new to commend it. A similar sort of piece is "Bewitched," which is described on the play-bill as "a new three-act farcial scream;" and in a note following the cast of characters the author, Mr. E. E. Kidder, acknowledges the quadruple inspiration of the novels of Messrs. Rider Haggard, Marion Crawford, Robert Louis Stevenson and F. Anstey. The remarkable popularity of these stories "has led the undersigned to believe that a play dealing with the merry side of occultism, and giving Mr. Russell ample scope for his acknowledged comedy talent, might create hilarity," and therefore Mr. Kidder has caused *Colonel Chutney Chillecurry* to return from India to London to the house of his cousin, *Mr. Euston*, and to bring – among other gifts for his relatives—a wonderful amulet. This Eastern charm works strange and often disastrous results upon any one who happens to have it in his possession ; the *Colonel* and his pretty daughter *Stella* are nearly wrecked on their homeward passage, and the carriage breaks down in carrying them from the ship to their cousin's house ; *Halcyon Todd*, a good young man, who is also a guest at the *Eustons'*, turns from extreme bashfulness and much reading of tracts by the Rev. Dodo Drake to the boldest flirtations and many other iniquities ; and the amulet brings about no end of unaccountable changes and droll situations. It is rather a pity, on the whole, that an actor who has so much of the genuine *vis comica* as belongs to Mr. Sol Smith Russell should seek no better vehicle for the exercise of his talents. "The Great Pink Pearl," in which Mr. William Gillette as well as Mr. E. H. Sothern has played the leading part, is of rather better quality than any of the plays yet named ; but

farce prolonged to the three acts of comedy is not
serious art, however much it may amuse for the
moment. The trouble with "The Great Pink Pearl,"
is that it is not continuously amusing, and it is hard
to understand why it should have been so successful
in London before its transplantation to America.
But it is a classic in comparison with some other
pieces of a light order which the season developed.
One of the worst of these was "My Brother's Sister,"
in which Miss Minnie Palmer essayed to amuse
theatre-goers. In the words of one distinguished
critic it was "sheer lunacy," and Miss Palmer's hard
and vulgar method was far from redeeming it.
"Upside Down," the work of Mr. J. J. McNally—
who is surely capable of better things—was apparently
written merely to display the acrobatic proclivities of
the Dalys, and so far it served its purpose. "Dollars
and Hearts," "Natural Gas" and "Little Puck" are
other efforts in the same line which occur to us as
examples of the utter imbecility of a certain portion
of the American drama.

So many of the minor plays of the season have been
touched upon in the article to which reference has
already been made, that the new pieces of a melodramatic or domestic order can be very briefly dismissed
here. "René," which was the *pièce de résistance* of
the Redmund-Barry Company, is a very old-fashioned
affair indeed. It is all red lights and tinsel, and naïve
to the point of absurdity in the almost primeval conditions which its *dramatis personæ* observe. Sir John
Millais's well-known painting, "The Huguenot,"

seems to have suggested the theme of the piece, for
the gallant lover is of the faction of Henri de Navarre,
while his mistress belongs (so far as her surroundings
go) to the other side. These two pose for the picture
in the course of the prologue, and the refusal of the
former to purchase safety by wearing the white scarf
leads naturally to the complications which follow.
The authorship of the piece is unknown—at least, it
is unacknowledged—but its literary merits are not such
as to make the question a pressing one. Mr. Redmund finds a congenial part in _René_, admirably suited
to his robust (and occasionally robustious) style ; and
the quality of manly sincerity which pervades his
work makes its comparatively prosaic character seem
for the moment to take on a touch of poetry. Mrs.
Barry was not particularly happy as the _Duchess
d'Armonville_, the mother of the young man with
whom _René_ fights. She could not help being impressive now and then, but her methods were curiously
hard and cold, and in her moments of intense passion
she was positively metallic. Of the rest of the company Mr. W. M. Fairbanks did excellent work in the
rather conventional guise of a cowardly sergeant. A
play of the most intense order is " Monbars," with
which Mr. Mantell filled out his second season as a
star. In the words of one critic, " It is a dreary melodrama, full of crudities and impossibilities, with a
villain to whom _Iago_ were an angel, a heroine to
whom spotless _Innocence_ herself were blemished, and
a husband of so sweet simplicity and confiding credulity that a baby prattler listening to fairly tales were
a marvel of shrewdness and sagacity in comparison.

All the crimes are desperately black, and on all the virtues white paint is lavished fathoms deep.   Scream after scream rent the startled air as the acts went on, and yell after yell sent the echoes flying   If the piece were handled with discretion and moderation it might be tolerated with patience, but Mr. Mantell's, methods are far too boisterous and vociferous, his contrasts are too abrupt, and too often he tears his passion to tatters. At times he strikes a strong note truly, and here and there he shows genuine pathos."   Another complicated melodrama is " The Golden Giant," in which Mrs. McKee Rankin appeared with some success.   It may be briefly described as the story of an innocent woman whom circumstances have driven into an appearance of guilt, of an honest man who suffers at the hands of the same persons that have been made the instruments of circumstance against the woman, and of a downright sort of girl, the course of whose true love runs roughly enough through three acts, but becomes satisfactorily smooth at last.   The plot need not be recited.   It is the clever use of a conventional scheme and incidents that are familiar to all students of Bret Harte.   Love and hate, ambition and revenge —even day-to-day chat—are all expressed in terms of poker, and before the curtain falls on the last scene of reconciliation, peace and happiness, the adaptable spectator begins to feel that he, too (with a little practice), might soon learn to speak the language of the game and the camp like any native.   The acting is better than the play, and Mrs. Rankin may be congratulated on her performance of *Bet*.   Her pathos is too complicated to be real, but happily *Bet's* pathos is infrequent ; and Mrs. Rankin, besides improving with a certain slangy grace all the opportunities for her droll and genuine humour, gives to more than one scene a very pretty dash of sentiment. Far worse from every point of view is Mr. Charles S. Gayler's "Lights and Shadows," in which villainy of every sort abounds, and Mr. James A. Herne's "Drifting Apart," which is interesting only as an example of the lengths to which unreality can go. Other new pieces, less melodramatic but very nearly as absurd, are "His Lordship" and "Parvenues," each produced in the spring at Brooklyn. Miss Estelle Clayton's new play, "A Sad Coquette," based upon Miss Rhoda Broughton's popular novel, "Good-bye, Sweetheart," though crude enough in many respects, is woven of essentially better stuff than most of these others. Mr. Gillette's revised version of his own play, "Held by the Enemy," makes it one of the best American plays of the season, and his own acting as the war correspondent and Miss Minnie Dupree's impersonation of *Susan McCreery* deserve an especial word of praise. The plays in which Miss Ullie Akerstrom made her appearance at the Boston Theatre deserve far less praise. But Miss Akerstrom herself made, on the whole, a very good impression. She has a graceful figure, an expressive and rather interesting face, and she plays with much quiet sincerity and freshness of style. But she has not yet attained either of those desirable qualities, force or finish. The best feature of her work is her remarkably pretty dancing.

EDITOR.

AMBITIOUS AMATEURS.

AT what precise point the amateur actress ceases
to be an amateur and becomes a "professional" is a
subject upon which reflection exercises itself with
perplexing results.   It would appear, on passing
thought, that when she adopts the stage as a means
of livelihood, her amateur days are over ; but such is
not the case, for actresses from the amateur fold
have been on the stage for years without losing that
peculiar quality of style which, at the outset, separated
them from the actress who has acquired proficiency in
her art by slow degrees, and has progressed gradually from the foot to the top of the histrionic ladder.
Of late, a belief has gained strength that the educa-
tion, the good breeding and the fine social polish of
the drawing-room are excellent qualifications for the
stage, and make a valuable stock in trade for the
aspirant to take with her into the profession ; but
experience has demonstrated, over and over again,
that the brilliant and intelligent woman of society
cannot step from the drawing-room to the stage and
become a fine actress because of the advantages her
social affiliations have bestowed upon her.   The great
actress is as likely to come from the home of igno-
rance and poverty as from the higher walks of life,
and the ranks of stage supernumeraries, or to be more

æsthetic, stage auxilliaries have furnished more famous artists than have the circles of the aristocracy.

From the days of Nell Gwynne to the present time, it is humble life that has given to the theatre the vast majority of its good artists; not only humble life, but ignorant and ill-bred humble life. Well-educated and well-bred men and women have done honour to the stage and to themselves by their genius; but these do not constitute the bulk of those who have distinguished themselves in theatrical art. Great actors, like poets, are born, not made, and but few have been either born or made in what is known as society. And even outside the boundaries of society, there is no record of an actress winning deserved repute in her art, who attempted to leap at once from incapacity to efficiency.

The ambitious amateur is formed both in and out of society. It seems so easy to act. You have only to bear yourself as you would in real life, and the thing is done! And just here, is the fallacy indulged in by professionals and amateurs alike. Miss Crummles thinks, when she has bestowed her own special individuality upon *Ophelia*, that she has interpreted the character, and failing to perceive that this individuality is not in accordance with the poet's conception, she proceeds to imprint it upon Juliet, *Desdemona*, and *Rosalind,* until there is a maximum of Miss Crummles and a minimum of Shakspere. She has been natural according to her views of her own personal nature, and cannot understand why anybody should find her uninteresting, common-place, unrefined, and unpoetic. She fails to com-prehend that we do not want Miss Crummles, but that we do want *Ophelia*; that presenting a realistic version of Miss Crummles is not acting *Ophelia* in a realistic manner. In fact, Miss Crummles's views of art are bounded by Miss Crummles's small com-prehension of human nature, coloured by an abound-ing confidence in herself as a human microcosm.

During the past season we have had various ex-amples of the ambitious amateur; three of whom have come from within the sacred precincts of soci-ety. Here is Mrs. Langtry, for example, who has achieved a handsome competency through her act-ing. We say through her acting, though it is to be presumed that it is to her character as a professional beauty and a certain notoriety she has achieved in that character, that her success is mainly owing. She has been on the stage for some years, and yet still remains the amateur she was when she began. Her intelligence, her good breeding, and her educa-tion in the best social manners, may be conceded; but they have done nothing towards making her an actress. She may be very graceful in a drawing-room, but she is exceedingly ungraceful on the stage. Her experience has enabled her to gain something in confidence, and she is a trifle less stiff in action than she was when she began; but she is not yet at home on the stage; her utterances have still the insincere ring of the amateur, speaking mechanically the words she has committed to memory; and artificiality still continues to do service for art. If she had begun at the foot of the ladder, it is doubtful if it was in her to achieve more than she has achieved ; for with every-thing in her favour, and after four or five years experi-ence, she remains almost as crude, as inartistic, and as lacking in all the essentials of style, as she was when she first trod the stage.   Her capacity to hold the mirror up to nature is very limited.   In fact, the mirror she holds up to nature reflects only Mrs. Langtry, and though her personality may be a very pleasing one, we at last weary of the persistent intrusion of this personal Mrs. Langtry, and yearn for something that shall vary the monotony, — for something of the character that the dramatist has drawn.   The ambitious amateur has won wealth without ceasing to be an amateur, while many able, experienced, and gifted artists look on with wonder, perhaps with dismay and envy, at the ease with which the success, for which they have toiled in vain, is gained by one without a tithe of their talent and natural aptitude for the stage.

The ambitious amateur from social circles must, however, have something more than her intelligence, her good breeding, and her art to offer the public. She must have a little history which shall attract the interest of the play-going community.   There must be a touching story of reduced circumstances, of romantic yearnings for distinction, of uncongenial married life, flavoured with a slight sauce of a piquant nature.   The public must be stimulated with a crav-ing to see her, not for her gifts, but for her notoriety. When this is done discreetly, the world will flock to see her as it flocks to see a famous prizefighter or any other passing popularity. The influence of this on the progress of dramatic art is unwholesome. It sets up mediocrity as an idol, and makes a religion of incapacity.

Another ambitious amateur from the salons of society is Mrs. James Brown Potter. She has as yet given no evidence of natural fitness for the stage. She is, perhaps, more interesting than Mrs. Langtry, owing to a finer grace of bearing, and higher delicacy of manner. As an amateur she outrivals her rival in point of efficiency, but an amateur she is, and to all appearances an amateur she will continue to be. Here, again, is art limited to the personality of the artist, and the nature of Mrs. Potter made to do full service for the nature of the various characters she assumes. It is always Mrs. Potter, with the same mild hysteria of style, the same unchanging expression of countenance, the same deliberate attitudinizing and the same woful, appealing elocution. Society has produced, no doubt, a very charming woman in her, but it has not produced an actress. Her success has not equalled that of Mrs. Langtry, but who knows what may come? Nothing was left undone to stimulate public interest in her. She began by horrifying society with readings of "Ostler Joe," no particularly sinful proceeding in itself, but a somewhat *risqué* business for a modest woman to be engaged in. It accomplished its purpose, however, and made her name familiar all over the land. Then came rumours that she was "going over" to the stage. These were denied and affirmed and re-denied and re-affirmed with amusing persistency to those who were at all worldly-wise. Then the subject of this sudden public interest went abroad, and was heard of as a favourite in exclusive London society. Then came stories of the interest of the Prince of Wales in the fair American, and then came a London appearance on the stage. The Prince of Wales applauded; the critics were more or less kind, and the new ambitious amateur was launched upon a theatrical career. All of this was piquant enough; but an additional piquancy was given, when the lady and her husband agreed to disagree, he objecting to her adopting the stage, and she resolutely insisting upon following the course upon which she had entered with so much of careful preparation. They separated, and the lady was fully equipped to court and to receive the favour of the public. She failed, however, to excite attention to the extent that Mrs. Langtry excited it. There was something of a twice-told tale in the enterprize. The Prince of Wales vein had been worked out by Mrs. Langtry, and she also had separated from her husband. The Potter proceeding looked very like a plagiarism. And yet Mrs. Potter is a better amateur actress than is Mrs. Langtry, and in this day of protection to home manufactures, patriotism should have made her success equal, at least, to that of her sister amateur.

Both ladies are doubtless inspired by a conscientious desire to win merited fame in the art they follow; but merited fame is not within their reach. They have leaped at once to accomplish what can only be done by years of study, backed by innate power. The stage should not be made at once a nursery and a hospital for the mistaken. It is fully time to enter a protest against ambitious amateurs, who insist upon putting themselves in the wrong place. The beginnings of an artistic career are interesting to watch when they are made by beginners in the positions in which they belong; but when the ordinary and the obviously proper course is reversed, and the beginner starts at the head of the class instead of the foot, showing unfitness and maintaining unfitness to occupy the place usurped, common sense would seem to indicate that something very like dignified rebuke would not be wholly out of order. In matters of art there should be no compromise between the good and the bad; and when that art is acting, there is a rank injustice in tolerating an incapacity in a society-petted amateur, that would meet with reprehension if manifested by a mediocre "professional." We live, however, in an era when toleration is not difficult of achievement if sufficient notoriety can be gained by the to-be-tolerated. Bad pictures and weak novels enjoy a large vogue, but the incompetent painters and the misguided authors are not accorded the consideration nor the position extended to the incompetent and misguided ambitious amateur actress. The dauber and the scribbler fall into their proper places, and criticism refuses to view them seriously; but the inefficient society actress continues to remain out of place, and criticism is painfully considerate of her.

Another type of the ambitious amateur is found in Miss Maude Banks. Here also a certain social

interest lent its glamour to the novice who essayed
to make one stride from the weak, semi-privacy of
recitation to the position of a theatrical star. The
results in her case were no more auspicious, as far
as genuine art success is concerned, than were those
in connexion with the amateurs already discussed.
Miss Banks is of the stage, stagey. In speech, gesture, and action, she exaggerates ; she has not gone to
nature to study ; she has not even gone to herself,
but she has studied directly from the stage, and the
consequence is a stilted and heavy insincerity in all
that she does. Her elocution is of the school of
oratory order, formal, artificial, and cold; without
one thrill of real emotion, and always suggesting to
the critical hearer a lesson committed to heart, and
repeated with zeal, but with self-consciousness and
perfunctory deliberation. Stiff and artificial in gesture, moving about the stage in a manner that never
once excites an impression of spontaneity in action,
but that always does excite the impression that her
motions have been carefully prepared in advance ;
mistaking noise for passion, and moan for pathos, she
represents amateur acting in its most conventional
phase. She may, with experience, grow into something more of an artist, but there are no indications
of genius in her work ; there is no frenzy of enthusiasm, the outcome of overabundant feeling, nothing
of that promising too-much that may be diminished,
and an excess of that too-little which requires almost
everything to be added. Miss Banks is another
instance, on a more modest level, of the uselessness
of education, society experience, and refinement of

manners in an artist when they are not backed up by a gift for the art adopted. She has been some two years on the stage, but, in common with Mrs. Langtry and Mrs. Potter, has made but little advance save in that greater self-possession and ease that come of familiarity with her work. Here, again, was a wrong beginning ; the attempt to run before she had learned to creep. The ambitious amateur will remain an amateur to the end. Genius and talent for the stage show themselves early ; they cannot be acquired. Routine may be achieved, but this is neither genius nor talent.

The ambitious amateur, however, is not wholly confined to society circles. There is Miss Margaret Mather, who after years of experience, and under the most favourable surroundings, remains essentially where she began. There was an accession from the ranks of humble life that suddenly appeared as a star, and, showing decided talent, obtained instant consideration from the more thoughtful. If she had entered a stock company in a modest position, and had learned her art step by step, there is every reason to believe that she would have made a mark, and have achieved a rank that would have been an honour to her. Nothing that could be done to stimulate public interest in her, and to win for her public favour, was left undone ; it only remained for her to justify the preparations that were made to smooth her way to merited success. Her earlier efforts were marked by fine flashes of power, but they were the efforts of an amateur. Her later efforts were marked by exactly the same flashes, which in due

season have become mannerisms, and her efforts are
still those of an amateur. The opening promise has
not been fulfilled; she has made, like the others, advances in the technical requirements of her art, but
in the finer intellectual qualities, in grasp of the language she speaks, in appreciating the character she
acts, in a keener knowledge of the deeper springs of
human nature, she has not advanced at all. Those
who have occupied our attention before, at least
speak their language with purity ; but Miss Mather's
pronunciation is far from correct, and is often vulgar.
We hear *Juliet* and *Rosalind* clipping their words,
abusing final syllables, and giving uncouth and provincial enunciation even to the simplest terms. In
action, nature is made to give way to staginess, and
in elocution, it is still the stage that rules. In the
other instances upon which we have dwelt, talent
was wanting ; in this instance there was talent
originally, but it was dwarfed and nullified for lack of
the proper training. The fatal top of the ladder
worked its accustomed woe. Mrs. Langtry, Mrs.
Potter, and Miss Banks, may possibly do better than
they have done; Miss Mather has reached the full
extent of her artistic development, and must remain
the ambitious amateur forevermore. Her gifts can
be pushed no further, and advertising has done all
that it can do for her.

This success of the amateur actress is a curious
commentary upon the taste of the day for acting.
We are not among those who believe that the stage
has fallen from its high estate into utter degeneracy,
but we are among those who believe that the critical

taste for acting has suffered something of an eclipse. When that taste demands imperatively something better than that which now gratifies or satisfies it that something better will appear in response to the call. It is not easy to believe that the reign of the ambitious amateurs can be a prolonged one. The public cannot tolerate in the dramatic art that against which they would protest vigorously if given to them in any other art. They cannot continue to receive crude and unfinished work, when they have once learned how crude and unfinished it is. They will undoubtedly continue to witness the growth of an artist, but the artist will be on that round of the ladder appropriate to the stage of development reached, and will not be permitted to develop at the top. Meanwhile, the way of the ambitious amateur is free from those thorns that beset the path of the professional artist of larger gifts; unless it be those critical thorns against whose prickings, social prestige, refinement of manners, puffery, and sensational advertising are as naught.

B. E. WOOLF.

THE END.

www.ingramcontent.com/pod-product-compliance
Lightning Source LLC
Chambersburg PA
CBHW021058030726
47496CB00006B/1902